Celebrate! VI

THE ANNUAL FOR CAKE DECORATORS

EDITED BY EUGENE T. AND MARILYNN C. SULLIVAN

Celebrate! VI

CO-EDITORS:
Marilynn C. Sullivan
and Eugene T. Sullivan

DECORATORS:
Michael Nitzsche, senior decorator
Amy Rohr and Dong Tuy Hoa

PRODUCTION ASSISTANT: Ethel LaRoche

READERS' EDITOR: Diane Kish

STAFF PHOTOGRAPHER: Edward Hois

DECORATING CONSULTANT: Norman Wilton
Special thanks are also given to
Norman Wilton for designing and
decorating the cakes shown on
pages 45, 46, 48, 49 and 51.

Second printing 20,000 July, 1981

Please address mail to:
    Wilton Book Division
    2240 West 75th Street
    Woodridge, Illinois 60515
Photographs and other material submitted for
publication must be accompanied by a stamped,
self-addressed envelope, if return is requested.

CELEBRATE!® VI
THE ANNUAL FOR CAKE DECORATORS
is published by Wilton Enterprises,
2240 West 75th Street, Woodridge, Illinois 60515

Library of Congress Catalog Card Number: 75-24148
International Standard Book Number: 0-912696-17-6

A WORD FROM THE PRESIDENT:

With *Celebrate! VI* Wilton brings you a star-studded galaxy of *all-new* decorated cakes. As you have come to expect, *Celebrate! VI* is a book of spectaculars—some that a novice can achieve, others a master will find challenging.

During the past year, thousands of you have written to tell us what you would like to see featured in *Celebrate! VI*. We have paid close attention to every suggestion. As a result, you will find that cake decorating truly takes on a *new* dimension in *Celebrate! VI*. You will be introduced to *new* ways to create beauty. You will be shown a number of *new* uses of tubes. You will also learn techniques *new* to decorators. To fulfill your requests, we've shown lots of *new* ways to use cake pans. And with many decorating projects in the book, you'll be let in on the "decorator's secret," a worthwhile tip on the better and easier way to work a bit of decorating magic.

We know you'll find *Celebrate! VI* one of the most stimulating books in your decorating library.

All of us at Wilton are constantly working on *new* products to make your decorating easier, faster, more beautiful and more fun.

With all our best wishes for happy decorating for years to come.

VINCENT A. NACCARATO
PRESIDENT, WILTON ENTERPRISES

The Celebration Year

Good news for readers

The Sugar Plum Shop

Practical information for decorators

Celebrate! VI

THE ANNUAL FOR CAKE DECORATORS

Dear Friends,

MAKE SOMEONE HAPPY is the theme of *Celebrate! VI.* You know, we decorators are lucky. It's so easy for us to use our skill and artistry to bring joy to others. There's something about the gift of a beautifully decorated cake that lifts the heart of the person who receives it, and that of the decorator, too.

All of us at the Wilton Book Division have devoted months of happy activity to decorating cakes that celebrate every month of the year. We've created lots of cakes that know no season, too—cakes that just say "you're so special." We hope that many of them will inspire you to create masterpieces of your own—and make someone happy.

As a special feature of *Celebrate! VI,* we've added "decorator's secrets" to many of our cake descriptions. If we've discovered an easier or quicker way to achieve an effect, we explain it to you. We share ways of arranging flowers, of mixing colors, of adapting a cake design to different occasions. As you leaf through this book, watch for these "secrets." I know they'll make your work easier and more enjoyable—and your cakes even prettier and more professional.

As a companion to *Celebrate! VI,* we've prepared the *Celebrate! VI Pattern Book.* It contains all the patterns you'll need to decorate any cake in this book.

My sincere thanks to all of you who have sent letters and notes. Your suggestions and comments have been immensely helpful to us. And of course, I welcome your opinions on this, our newest book.

Welcome to *Celebrate! VI!* I hope it will give you many years of enjoyment in the happy art of cake decorating.

NORMAN WILTON

Celebrate!

JANUARY AND FEBRUARY

It's almost midnight!
Directions, page 7

hello to a Happy New Year!

MAKE SOMEONE HAPPY!
That's a wonderful New Year's resolution—and one very easy for a decorator to carry out! You don't need to be reminded of the joy a decorated cake brings, so use your talent to spread happiness every week of the year. Decorate a party cake, a birthday cake, a holiday cake, or a just-to-say-you're-special cake and present it to someone dear. This book is full of happy cakes to inspire your efforts. Watch the smiles and you'll get back a happy feeling, too!

Say it in Vietnamese

February 16 is New Year's day in Vietnam. A sheet cake adorned with a brilliant greeting and a mock-ferocious dragon sets a unique theme for a jolly New Year party. To list all the meanings that the dragon motif holds in Oriental art would require a book of at least this size! The dragon controls rain and is therefore important for a fruitful crop. He is the guardian of treasures, especially precious stones. He is the emblem of good and wise government—no wonder dragons are painted on porcelain, woven into silk, carved in stone and wood.

1. Our dragon is made in the Color Flow technique. Tape *Celebrate! VI* pattern to stiff board or glass and tape wax paper smoothly over it. Outline the design with tube 1, let crust, then fill in areas with thinned Color Flow icing. (Recipe is on package.) When the dragon is completely dry, outline again with tube 1s and pipe the scales and other details.

2. Bake and fill a two-layer 9″ x 13″ sheet cake. Cover with rolled fondant as described on page 52. Pipe a tube 10 ball border at base and trim with

tube 2 string and dots.

3. The fill-in method is used for the decorative lettering. Transfer pattern to cake and outline with a mixture of half piping gel, half royal icing and tube 1. Let outlines dry, then fill in with piping gel mixed with enough water to flow easily from a cone with a tiny cut tip. Carefully place dragon on cake and serve to 24 guests.

It's almost midnight!
Shown on page 5

Make this quaint cuckoo clock for your New Year's Eve celebration and charm your guests! The clock is constructed of cake and gingerbread with delicious marzipan trim and a fillip of miniature pretzels.

1. Use *Celebrate! VI* patterns to cut out gingerbread roof and gable pieces. (Recipe page 158.) Bake and cool and mark roof pieces for scallops. Make a recipe of marzipan and tint brown, red and green and a tiny portion yellow. Leave a small amount untinted. Roll out about ⅛″ thick and cut bird house, hearts and clock face from patterns, leaves with small ivy leaf cutter, flowers with forget-me-not cutter. Dry leaves within curved form, other pieces flat. Join double pieces with egg white. Hand-model the cuckoo, shown here actual size, and pipe beak and eyes with tube 1. Glaze all marzipan pieces, then pipe clock numbers and beading with tube 2. Using pattern, make a paper flag, letter with tube 1 and glue to a toothpick.

2. Bake three 8″ square layers and fill to achieve a height of 6″. Ice with buttercream. Use *flat ribbon tube ID* to outline each side. This tube pipes a bold effect in a hurry! Pull up a tube 20 shell from each corner, then add

tube 2 beading. Pipe a tube ID line at top edges of two gable pieces. Pipe tube 2 stems on all four sides of cake.

3. Mound icing on cake top at front and back and set gables in position. Do the same on other two sides and carefully place roof sections on gables. Pipe a line of icing where roof sections meet. Hold for a moment to set. Pipe zigzag scallops on roof with tube 2. Attach birdhouse, clock face, ivy leaf and flower trim to clock with icing. Ice heart-shaped "door" to a toothpick and attach in open position. Insert a toothpick for cuckoo's perch and attach bird. Finish by securing pretzels to roof with icing and inserting flagpole. Just as cute as it can be! Serves 16 with gingerbread a bonus for nibbling.

Decorator's secret. Would you like a larger cake to serve a crowd? Set the cuckoo clock on a 12″ or larger square cake.

Fragile fine line tracery

The smallest tubes create the most artistic effects! In the Continental fine line style, repeated curved borders and delicate motifs are piped on cakes with round tubes 000, 1s or the smaller tubes in the "L" series. Use thinned royal icing for this work to make the piped lines effortless—we mixed ¼ tablespoon piping gel and one tablespoon royal icing and used a tiny parchment cone. Patterns are in the *Celebrate! VI Pattern Book* but use them mainly for practice. Cover

with wax paper and trace over the designs until your hand becomes accustomed to the curves and lines—then do most of the piping freehand.

Since Continental cakes are harmonious in their flavors, use a chocolate recipe and filling for the square cake, and flavor the batter and filling for the round cake with raspberry or cherry. Poured fondant makes a perfect background for the delicate designs.

A chocolate valentine

1. Pipe tube 103 buttercream roses and freeze or air-dry.

2. Cover a two-layer 8″ square cake with glossy chocolate poured fondant. Ice a heart cupcake with pink poured fondant and set in center of cake. Pipe name with tube 1s and beading with tube 3. Pipe tube 3 stems, arrange roses and add tube 65 leaves. Mark sides of cake with dots for pattern position.

3. Use tube 000 for all piping. Make a series of looped dropped strings around top edge, then scallops below them. Add dots and tiny hearts. Pipe side motifs with a continuous gliding line, then pipe "e's" between them and add dots. Finish with a tube 6 ball border at base. Serve this Continental creation to twelve guests.

A lacy valentine

1. Pipe buttercream roses with tube 103, forget-me-nots with tube 101s. Air-dry or freeze. Cover a two-layer 10" cake with poured fondant. Mark lattice heart on top center. Mark dots 1" apart on top edge to indicate center of hearts. Mark a ¾" strip around cake near base to guide lattice.

2. Pipe all trim with tube 000 and thinned royal icing. Fill in large heart area with fine line lattice. Drop double scallops around heart and finish with dots and tiny hearts. Drop heart-and-string border from top edge, starting with centers of hearts. Drop double strings and add fleurs-de-lis and dots below.

Fill the marked strip with lattice and pipe a tube 6 base border. Arrange flowers on cake top and trim with tube 65s leaves. Serve to 14.

Decorator's secret. Learn much more about this fascinating technique in Chapter Four, *The Wilton Way of Cake Decorating, Volume III.*

What makes a *Pretty* cake *Quick* to decorate?

Decorators love a challenge! They're eager to learn new skills, try new techniques, create real masterpieces. But decorators are also very busy people who often need to turn out a pretty cake in next-to-no time. Here are a few secrets from our staff to help speed your decorating and achieve a cake you'll be proud of.

SIMPLE CONSTRUCTION. When you're in a hurry, don't think in terms of pillars, separator plates, dowels for support. (An exception would be a separator set whose legs just push into the cake and provide their own support.) Don't attempt a cake that requires cutting to shape or constructing from several shapes.

A LIMITED COLOR SCHEME. Save the cakes that use a rainbow of tinted icings for the days when you have plenty of time. Plan on using just two or three colors—but make sure that they are pleasing and pretty. Often you can tint your colors progressively. See page 134 for method.

QUICK PATTERNING. Avoid designs that require transferring patterns, or very careful measuring. Instead, depend on easy divisions you can do with your eye. Almost any area can quickly be divided into fourths, then into eighths or more without measuring. And use pattern presses or cookie cutters to mark an elaborate-looking design in an instant.

JUST A FEW TUBES can decorate a cake very quickly and save you the time needed to change them—and wash them later! Don't overlook the time-saving convenience of a coupler. By attaching one to a purchased decorating bag you can change tubes in a flash without changing bags.

Star tubes are fast tubes! They produce a multitude of curving sculptural forms very quickly.

READY-MADE PROPS. Add a cute little plastic figure to a child's cake, a lacy umbrella to a shower cake, a dainty bassinet to a christening cake. With such a variety of novel trims available you'll find it easy to produce an appealing cake without too much piped decoration. Candles, too, add life and sparkle.

MADE-AHEAD TRIMS. This is perhaps the most time-saving tip of all. Make a habit of piping flowers with any icing left over as you complete a decorating project. Take an hour or two when you have leisure to pipe some trays of flowers. You'll improve your decorating skills and have a garden of blooms all ready to trim a cake on a busy day. Royal icing flowers can be stored indefinitely in covered boxes. Store buttercream flowers in your freezer.

ORGANIZE! Decorate the cake in the proper progression for professional results. This usually means first make necessary trims, then bake and ice the cake, and lastly, pipe borders and trims. For almost all cakes, start at the bottom and work up.

Keep your tools well organized, too. Set aside a shelf or two where everything can be stored neatly—boxes of flowers, well labeled, spatulas, tubes, pans and everything else you use in decorating. On a rushed day you'll avoid a lot of panic when everything you need is at hand.

AT LEFT are two sweet examples of pretty valentine cakes that can be decorated very quickly. Make one of them for someone you love.

You're just super!

And so is this love cake. Trim it with just two tubes, a pair of lovebirds and a paper heart.

1. Trace a heart-shaped cookie cutter about 4″ high on red construction paper, cut it out and write your message with tube 2. Add scallops.

2. Bake a two-layer 12″ round cake. Fill and ice with buttercream. Make a mark on top edge of cake and one directly opposite it. Make two more marks midway between the first two, dividing cake in fourths. Lightly imprint a 2½″ heart cutter at these points, then press two hearts between each for a total of twelve. Press cutter on side of cake, using heart designs on top as guides.

3. Pipe base shell border with star tube 22. Outline hearts on side, then top of cake with tube 18. Add stars at points of hearts and at top edge with tube 22. Set lovebirds on cake top, trim with a few made-ahead roses and paper heart. Serve to 22.

Light of my life

1. Bake, fill and ice a two-layer 9″ x 13″ sheet cake. Also bake and ice a single-layer 6″ round tier. Lightly mark the center of the sheet cake with a 6″, then an 8″ cake circle or pan.

2. Using marked circles as guide, pipe tube 2 scallops, outer curves touching 8″ circle. Pipe a second series of scallops within the first and finish with dots. Pipe plump red hearts within scallops with tube 6. (Two shell shapes, touching.) Set 6″ tier on sheet cake.

3. Pipe tube 10 base bulb border, tube 8 border at top. Edge top and bottom of round tier with tube 6. Write your message with tube 2, then add more hearts, using tube 8 for sides of sheet cake, tube 6 for 6″ tier. Insert two slender tapers, each tied with a bow. Serve to 27 guests.

Quick and Pretty Valentines

to decorate for your love

Aren't these the most beguiling love cakes you've ever seen? They're lavished with lace, hearts and flowers and fluffy swirls of icing—but each is quick to do. Boiled icing is used for all borders—it's very easy to pipe with.

Victorian valentine

Lacy fans are the show-off trim on this cake for a big party. It's so pretty you won't need any other centerpiece.

1. Pipe the roses ahead with tubes 104 and 125. Make ½" accordion pleats in three 12" square paper doilies. Fold each in half, insert a toothpick in the fold, then tape to make a fan.

2. Bake, fill and ice the two-layer tiers—a 12" square and an 8" round. Assemble. Pipe a row of puffy shells around the base of the bottom tier with tube 18. Pipe garlands at top edge of tier and little hearts between each with tube 14. Drop tube 2 string over garlands. Do reverse shell top border with tube 16. On upper tier, pipe base shell border with tube 17 and trim with tube 2 scallops. Top border matches one on base tier.

Now attach the fans by inserting toothpicks into the tiers and heap roses at their bases. Serves 46.

Sweetheart valentine

Sparkling sugar hearts are the appropriate trim on this sweet little cake.

1. Mold two of them in the heart cupcake pan, hollow out, and attach back-to-back with a popsicle stick between them with royal icing. Page 33 gives method. Write message with tube 2 and edge with tube 14 shells. Mold the little hearts in candy molds.

Attach six of them back-to-back with a toothpick between. Pipe drop flowers with tube 96.

2. Bake and ice a cake in the hexagon ring pan. The shape makes the decorating almost automatic. Pipe all the swirls and fleurs-de-lis with tube 96. This drop flower tube pipes outstanding borders! Cut a circle from 2" styrofoam to fit hole in cake, ice and place in hole. Insert large and small hearts, bouquet fashion. Finish the trim by securing hearts and flowers to cake side and piping a few tube 65 leaves. Serve to twelve.

Flowery valentine

This little square cake makes use of a pretty shortcut for the top trim.

1. Stripe the inside of a decorating cone with deep pink icing and fill with lighter pink. Pipe tube 103 sweet peas.

2. Bake and fill a two-layer 8" square cake. Ice with *boiled icing*. Mark four heart shapes on top of cake with a 3" cutter. Write message with tube 2. Now thin food coloring with water to a deep pink and paint the heart areas with an artist's brush. Note: the cake must be covered with boiled icing for this technique. Cover the areas with Philippine lacework as described on page 65. Outline the hearts with tube 33, ending with a fleur-de-lis at each corner. Complete the trim by piping tube 35 curved shells at the base of cake and forming cascades with the flowers. Serves twelve.

Decorator's secret. This painting technique gives a showy trim in a hurry! Philippine lace is very fast.

Here's to an exciting New Year!

Here's a New Year's cake with all the swirling color and excitement of a Chinese street parade! Create this scaly dragon, breathing fire, lashing his tail and glaring from his blood-red eyes. Set him on a sheet cake—children will give delighted shrieks and grown-ups will gaze in open-mouthed astonishment.

How to build a dragon

He's really a sweetheart—start with a cake baked in a ring mold and add marshmallows, buttercream and summer coating triangles for his jagged spine! Bake a single layer in a 12″ x 18″ sheet cake pan for the base. The picture shows how to begin.

1. Prepare green summer coating as described on page 146. Spread to ⅛″ thickness on smooth foil and let set up. Cut triangles with a sharp knife, 1″ at base and about 1¼″ high. Trim off bases of four or five triangles to use for tail and neck areas.

2. Measuring on outer curve of ring cake, cut off a 7″ and a 2″ piece. Set cake on a 12″ x 18″ cake base and reconstruct. Reverse the curve of the 7″ piece and place in position for head and front of body. Taper the front as pictured. Reverse the curve of the 2″ piece and place for tail, slicing to taper as shown. Lightly outline cake on base, remove cake and cut out base on outlines. Re-assemble cake pieces on prepared base, joining with buttercream.

Marshmallows in two sizes and toothpicks do the rest. Three marshmallows form each sprawling leg, more build up the spine and make the lashing tail. Form open jaws with four large marshmallows, shape eyes and bumps on nose with small marshmallows.

3. Cover the dragon with buttercream. Round out form with tube 8 and smooth. Pipe lines around jaws, eyes and nostrils with tube 6. Spatula-stripe a cone with deep green icing and fill with lighter green. Cover the face with tube 13 stars and pull out scales on the body and legs with tube 83. This square-cut *specialty tube* makes the scales on the dragon very realistic!

Complete the picture

1. Ice the sheet cake, place on cake board and run a tube 6 line around base. On top of line, pipe *specialty tube 353* bamboo border. Hold this crescent-shaped tube at a 45° angle, curved side up. Run along with even pressure, pausing at intervals to let icing build up and form bamboo joints. Pipe the same border at top edge.

2. Set dragon, on its base, on sheet cake. Complete the trim with royal icing. Pull out tongue, ends of tail and fire-y halo with tube 17. Pipe tube 12 toes, then tube 6 claws and teeth. Whiskers extending from mouth are piped with tube 6, dried, then attached. Glaze eyes with corn syrup and the fire-breathing creature is complete! Cut him in 10 servings, sheet cake into 27 slices.

Decorator's secret. Use your imagination and pans you already have in your cupboard to create unique new cakes!

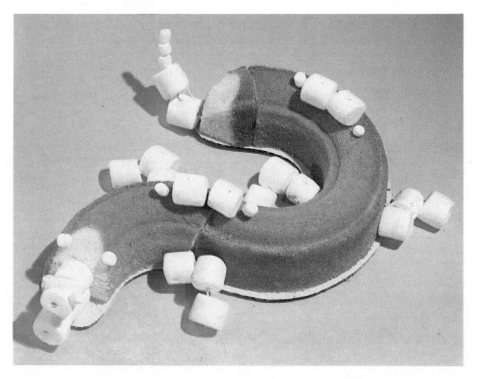

15

decorator's dream...the Tier Cak

There's no greater thrill for a decorator than to complete a towering tier cake. These lofty confections have an architectural beauty and importance no other cake can achieve. Yet, step by step, a tier cake is no more difficult to decorate than a series of smaller cakes.

Here's a little refresher course to remind you of the safe, sure way to construct a tier cake.

Prepare the tiers

Decide on the tier sizes and shapes, and design of your cake. This depends largely on the number of guests to be served (see page 22).

1. BAKE THE TIERS. To make sure they are level, swirl the batter from the center to sides of pan. Pin strips of damp toweling around pan sides. If baked layers are still not level, even them off with a serrated knife *after chilling*. Always chill or freeze the layers—they'll be much easier to handle. Thaw frozen layers an hour or so before icing.

2. BEFORE ICING, attach a cardboard cake base, same size and shape, to bottom layer. Use a little royal icing or corn syrup as glue. This base prevents knife scratches and makes it easy to move the tier. Pipe a ring of icing around edge of bottom layer, then spread filling (any recipe you like, except fresh fruit or a very perishable mixture). The ring of icing will keep the filling within the layers. Place top layer in position. Brush off loose crumbs.

3. CRUMB-COAT the tiers. Do this by brushing on *Apricot Glaze* (heat apricot jam to boiling, strain and brush on tier while hot). Or cover tier with a thin layer of icing. Let glaze or icing crust.

4. ICE THE TIERS, usually with buttercream. We recommend using a turntable. Spread icing on sides first, then heap on top and spread. Use plenty of icing and long spatula strokes. Smooth top by pulling a long metal ruler toward you. Smooth sides by holding spatula against tier and slowly spinning turntable. Now tiers are ready to assemble.

All tier cakes need support

Filled and iced tiers are heavy, so each needs a system of support to support the tier or tiers above. There are three ways to give this support.

1. Lift tiers with Clear Dividers that push into the tier.

2. Build tiers on the Tall Tier stand. A center column supports plates to hold the tiers.

3. Dowel support is the classic method used with your choice of pillars and plates.

FIRST SET BASE TIER on a sturdy cake board (four layers of cardboard covered with foil), or on a serving tray. Diameter of board or tray should be 4" larger than that of tier. Attach tier with strokes of royal icing or corn syrup.

The easiest support — Clear Dividers

Fit legs into separator plates for all upper tiers. (Choose plates 2" larger than diameter of tiers.) Attach tiers to plates. Hold middle tier, on plate, above base tier, making sure it is centered. Gently push legs through base tier until they touch cake board or tray. Assemble upper tiers the same way, *making sure legs line up.* Now you're ready to decorate. The first step is to measure and mark the tiers. Clear dividers give a sparkling, airy look.

Time to Celebrate!

A tier cake needn't be a wedding cake—here three sunny tiers spell out a greeting for the new year. The decorating is very simple, but the cake looks impressive because of the height provided by clear dividers.

1. Make the cheerful daisies in advance. Cover a number 8 nail with foil and pipe petals with tubes 103 and 102 and royal icing. The nail gives the petals a perky curve. Pipe centers with tube 4 and dry.

2. Bake three two-layer round tiers, 14", 10" and 6". Fill, ice and set each on a matching cake circle. Assemble with clear dividers. Divide and mark side of base tier in twelfths, side of middle tier in sixteenths and top tier in eighths.

3. Remove dividers and two upper tiers. Mark an 8-petal daisy design on top of base tier. Outline design with tube 18, adding shells at points. Cluster daisies in center of tier. Replace dividers and upper tiers. Do base shell border with tube 22, then add string, shells and stars and reverse shell top border with tube 18.

On middle tier pipe a tube 18 shell border at base. Do rest of decorating with tube 17. On top tier, pipe all trim with tube 17.

Pipe a mound of icing on top tier to support New Year's Eve clock. Arrange daisies around it and around dividers on middle tier. This impressive party centerpiece serves 56.

Decorator's secret. For a graceful, natural look, pose some of the flowers on small and large marshmallows iced to the tiers. Conceal them with other flowers.

The Tall Tier stand ...quick way to construct a tier cake

Here's another fast efficient way to build your dream cake. Select plates from the Tall Tier stand set to hold your tiers. Each plate should be 2" larger in diameter than the tier.

1. Before attaching the bottom layer of a tier to its cake base, cut a hole the diameter of the center post in the exact center of the cardboard base. Check to be sure hole is large enough for center column to slip through. Secure layer to base, then fill the layers. Now cut a hole in the exact center of the tier with the Cake Corer. Crumb-coat and ice the tier. Do the same for all tiers. Note: Do not cut a hole in the top tier.

2. Set all tiers, except top tier, on their plates and assemble by screwing in columns. Secure plate for top tier to column by screwing in nut, then place top tier in position. Measure and mark the tiers and start to decorate.

If you plan to do piping on tops, remove plates, with tiers, and set on cake pans to steady as you pipe top trims. Re-assemble the tiers and finish decorating.

The Tall Tier stand is very flexible— you can construct a many-tiered creation on it, or a more modest, two-tiered cake, as pictured at left. You can even add a four-arm unit to the center column to hold satellite cakes.

A dainty love cake with traditional heart-shaped trims

Be-ruffled and strewn with blossoms, this sweet tier cake makes a sentimental centerpiece for a big valentine celebration—or decorate it for an engagement announcement or the wedding itself. The Tall Tier stand makes construction easy.

1. Make trims ahead of time. First pipe many royal icing drop flowers with tubes 15, 225 and 131. Add tube 1 centers and dry. For ten curved hearts on lower tier, tape *Celebrate! VI* patterns to middle size of Flower Formers. Tape wax paper smoothly over them and outline designs with tube 14. Dry, then attach flowers with dots of icing and trim with tube 349 leaves. For top heart ornament, glue a 4" filigree heart to a petite ornament plate. Cut 3" squares of tulle and push centers into heart openings to form poufs. Attach flowers and pipe tube 349 leaf trim.

2. Bake the tiers. Bottom tier consists of a 12" round layer plus a 12" top bevel. Upper tier is an 8" round layer plus 8" top bevel. Fill layers, set on prepared cardboard bases and cover with marzipan, then rolled fondant. (See page 52 for method.) You will need 1½ recipes of the fondant. Assemble tiers on Tall Tier stand using 10" and 16" plates to accommodate bottom border on base tier. Make hole in bottom tier *after* it is covered with fondant. Divide bottom tier in tenths and mark on side 2½" up from base. Divide upper tier in eighths and mark 2" up from base.

3. Pipe tube 33 shells at base of lower tier and trim with tube 104 ruffles. Drop string guidelines, then pipe fluted ruffles on side with tube 103, leaving 1" between each curved ruffle. Trim on top tier is similar to bottom tier. Use tubes 21 and 104 for base border, 102 for side ruffle and 101s for bows.

4. Attach flowered hearts to bevel slant on bottom tier with dots of icing. Ring column with flowers and form clusters between scallops. Form a ring of flowers at top of upper tier and trim all flowers with tube 349 leaves. Set ornament in place and serve to 32 party guests. At a wedding reception, lower tier serves 68, upper tier 30.

Decorator's secret. To pipe the neat fluted ruffles, hold the petal tube with wide end against tier side, narrow end straight out. Move hand in a tight zigzag motion.

Supporting tiers with dowels and pillars

This is the classic method of tier construction, developed many years ago at Wilton. With this method you can be assured that your cake will stand securely—tall, straight and proud at the reception.

It's a very versatile method, too. You can use it for stacked tiers, for a cake like the one at right where the two lower tiers are stacked and the top tier lifted by pillars, or for a cake with many tiers, each separated by pillars.

With dowel construction you may choose from many styles and heights of pillars too. In describing dowel construction, we'll use the anniversary cake at right as an example. First secure the iced base tier to its serving tray or a sturdy cake board, 2" larger all around. (Stroke royal icing or corn syrup on board to secure.)

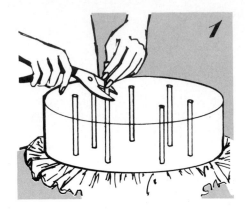

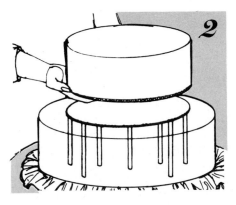

1. Lightly press a 10" cake circle or pan to the top of the base tier to mark a circle. Within this circle, insert eight ¼" dowel rods pushing each right down to the tray or cake board. Lift up and clip off level with surface of cake, then push down again.

2. Wrap a 12" cake circle (same size as middle tier) with clear plastic and lay on base tier. Set middle, 12" tier on it, securing with icing or syrup. Mark top of tier with an 8" circle. (Note that marked circle is smaller than separator plate.) Within marked circle insert six ¼" dowels, just as you did for the base tier. Clip off level with surface.

Sharpen a long dowel rod and push pointed end clear through both base and middle tiers, right down to tray or cake board. Clip off level with surface. This keeps tiers from swaying.

3. Attach pegs that come with plate to the bottom of a 10" plate and snap pillars in position. Center plate on tier and gently push down to tier surface.

4. Set top tier on second 10" plate (secure with icing or corn syrup) and attach to top of pillars.

Here is a rule of thumb: the larger and more numerous the tiers, the more dowels within each tier you will need for support. For a very large and heavy cake, use ½" dowels in the base tier.

Now you are ready to mark divisions on your assembled tiers and to proceed with decorating.

Directions for decorating the lovely anniversary cake pictured at right are on page 23. Use the same design for an outstanding wedding cake.

How many guests will your tier cake serve?

If your cake is planned for a wedding reception, as most tier cakes are, it is customary to serve dainty slices, approximately *two layers high, 1" wide and 2" deep.* The following chart will show you the number of servings to expect from each tier. If you prefer larger servings, cut the listed number of servings in half, and slice the pieces 2" wide.

Remember the top tier is usually frozen for the first anniversary, so do not include it in your calculations.

shape	size	servings
round	6″	16
	8″	30
	10″	48
	12″	68
	14″	92
	16″	118
	18″	148
square	6″	18
	8″	82
	10″	50
	12″	72
	14″	98
	16″	128
	18″	162
hexagon	6″	6
	9″	22
	12″	50
	15″	66
petal	6″	8
	9″	20
	12″	44
	15″	62
heart	6″	12
	9″	28
	12″	48
	15″	90

Do you like the design of a cake but need more servings than it will provide? Use one of these methods. First, add another base tier. Second, increase the size of all tiers by 2". If the original design calls for tiers 14", 10" and 6" in diameter, change the sizes to 16", 12" and 8". Thirdly, add two, four or more "satellite cakes"— 8", 10" or 12" cakes arranged around the main tier cake.

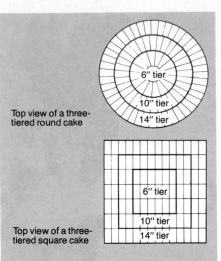

Top view of a three-tiered round cake

Top view of a three-tiered square cake

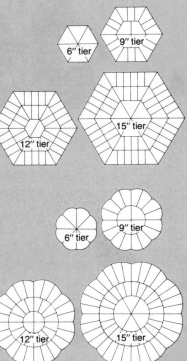

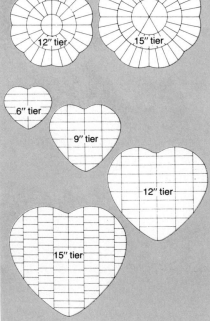

How to cut a tier cake

The rule is, start at the top and work down, separating each tier as you go. This rule applies to any tier cake, whether stacked or pillared.

FOR A ROUND-TIERED cake, first remove the top tier and set aside. Remove pillars and plate from top of next tier. Detach this tier from main cake. Make a circular cut 2" in from tier edge and cut 1" slices from it. Move in another 2", make a second cut and again cut 1" slices. Continue until tier is completely cut. Cut remaining tiers in the same fashion.

SQUARE TIERS. Remove and set aside top tier. Detach each tier before cutting, just as for round tiers. Move 2" in from one edge, cut a strip and cut 1" slices from it. Continue until tier is completely cut. Move to next lower tier.

CUT HEXAGON AND PETAL tiers like round tiers.

FOR HEART-SHAPED tiers, first cut the heart into vertical strips about 2" wide. Cut strips into 1" slices.

GROOM'S CAKES are cut in the same fashion as wedding cakes.

How to carry a tier cake

If the cake is constructed with pillars, clear dividers or on the Tall Tier stand, here is a foolproof method. Cut 3"- or 4"-thick soft foam into squares somewhat larger than the diameter of the tiers. Carve a depression in each foam square about 1" or 1½" deep, the shape and size of the separator plate. Take the tiers apart and set each, on its plate, in the depression. Cover each tier with light plastic (a cleaner's bag is fine) and place in the back of your station wagon. If you are carrying the cake in a car, you must have a platform built to level the back seat. Re-assemble the cake at the reception site.

A stacked cake is simply set into one foam square.

A summary of tier cake tips

FIRST DECIDE ON SERVINGS. If the design you like serves too few or too many, alter it as described at left.

DECIDE ON TYPE OF TIER SUPPORT. If you are really in a hurry, use clear dividers or the Tall Tier stand. Pillar-and-dowel construction takes a little longer but allows you the flexibility of choosing among many styles and heights of pillars.

WORK IN ORDER. If you do your work in orderly steps you will achieve a professional looking cake with no crises of nerves. For most tier cakes, this means first make flowers and other trims, then prepare and ice the tiers, assemble and finally do the decorating itself.

PREPARE THE TIERS carefully. Make sure they are level, and smoothly iced. No amount of decoration will hide an uneven, poorly iced tier.

START AT THE BOTTOM tier for the actual decorating, and work your way up, tier by tier. This is most practical for almost every tier cake.

START AT THE TOP when cutting and serving the cake.

ENJOY! A tier cake is just a series of smaller cakes. Decorate each tier carefully and discover the thrill of completing an architectural masterpiece, as lovely as a little temple!

FOR MORE INFORMATION on wedding cakes and how to design and decorate them, see *Beautiful Bridal Cakes the Wilton Way*. There are scores of full-color portraits of bridal and groom's cakes, too.

Mark an anniversary
shown on page 21 and at right

Were they married in January? Decorate this lavish tier cake to celebrate their anniversary, and trim it with carnations, January's flower.

1. Roll out gum paste ⅛" thick and cut ovals, support, and heart using

Celebrate! VI patterns. Dry heart on 16" curved form, other pieces flat. Trim large oval for top ornament with tube 14 shells and number, tube 18 fleur-de-lis. Secure Twin Angels with a small piece of gum paste dipped in egg white. Attach triangular support to oval base the same way, and add a 1½" strip of gum paste in front of support. Edge smaller oval with tube 13 and write names with tube 2. On heart, pipe tube 2 beaded edge and script.

2. Pipe royal icing carnations. Pipe a tube 12 ball on a number 9 nail. Stiffen icing and pipe tube 104 ruffled petals with a jiggling motion, starting at top center. Pipe a few flowers on florists' wire stems. First make a tube 12 calyx, dry and pipe a ball on top of it. Dry, then pipe petals. (Page 113.) Pipe tube 67 leaves on wires.

3. Bake, fill and ice two-layer tiers 16", 12" and 8." Make layers for two lower tiers 2" high, for top tier, 1½" high. Assemble with 5" Corinthian pillars and 10" plates, using dowel method, page 20. Divide 8" tier in eighths, 12" and 16" tiers in twelfths.

4. *On bottom tier,* secure heart to center front with icing. Pipe and over-pipe scrolls with tube 16. Do bottom border with tube 19, top border with tube 17. *On middle tier,* pipe scroll and fleur-de-lis design with tube 17. Use tube 19 for base border, tube 17 for top border. *On top tier,* pipe base shell border with tube 16. Use the same tube for the side trim. Pipe zig-zag scallops with a scroll below each. Add fleurs-de-lis, then over-pipe the scallops with a tube 13 line. Add a tube 16 top shell border.

5. Secure large oval to support with small balls of gum paste dipped in egg white. Attach smaller oval to pillar the same way and add a plastic Angelino at base. Arrange flowers, securing with icing, and trim with leaves. Serve wedding cake-sized pieces of two lower tiers to 186. The top tier is for the anniversary couple.

A New Year's greeting

1. Make the beautiful see-through design with the Color Flow technique. Tape *Celebrate! VI* pattern to a stiff surface, then tape wax paper smoothly over it. Do all outlining with tube 2 and Color Flow icing. Let outline crust. Thin the icing and flow in areas with a cone with a tiny cut tip. Dry, then over-pipe the outlines of "Peace" with tube 1. Dry again, then turn design over, peel off wax paper, and strengthen the design on the reverse side with tube 13 zigzags. Dry again.

2. Bake a two-layer 10" square cake, each layer about 2" high. Fill and ice with buttercream. Mark a 7" circle on cake top. To raise the Color Flow design, pipe a tube 6 line around circle, let dry, then over-pipe with a second line.

Pipe a curving tube 3 vine around the sides of the cake, then pipe short stems and add tubes 68 and 65 leaves. Pipe shell-motion borders with *leaf tube 68*. Fill in the circle with tube 3 and piping gel. Let the gel set, then add a second layer for rippled effect. Pipe a few dots of icing on the circle, and carefully place Color Flow design. Lift off before serving to 20 guests.

Decorator's secret. Here's how to remove a Color Flow design from wax paper. With a sharp knife, cut through the paper all around. Lay a piece of soft foam over the design, a piece of stiff cardboard over that. Invert this "sandwich" and design will rest on foam, wrong side up. Carefully peel off paper. Reverse the procedure to put design in right-side-up position.

Celebrate! ®

MARCH AND APRIL

An Easter centerpiece
Directions, page 26

An Easter centerpiece
shown on page 25

Have the fun of creating this pretty tableau in gum paste—and make everyone smile at seeing it Easter morning.

1. MOLD THE EGG over the two-piece egg pan. Use Philippine gum paste (page 159) for this to give strength. Roll out the gum paste in large ovals about ³/₁₆″ thick and smooth over the pans. Trim off at edges with a sharp knife. Trim about 1″ off the larger ends of the half-eggs for a base. To define four oval openings, press with a 4½″ plastic egg mold and cut out. Dry about 24 hours.

2. PREPARE THE BASE. Use the metal forget-me-not cutter to stamp out many flowers. (Wilton gum paste, page 158, is best for all trims.) Lay them on a piece of soft foam and press each in center with the round end of a modeling stick to curve. Add tube 2 royal icing centers and dry.

Cut out 16 leaves with the lily leaf cutter from The Flower Garden set.

Brush the top of a heart ornament base with egg white and lay the wet leaves on the base, curling up the tips. Attach flowers to the lower part of the base with royal icing and trim with tube 65 leaves.

Cut out a 4″ circle from 1″ thick styrofoam, taper to a saucer shape, ice with royal icing and cover with green gum paste. This will fit within egg as a foundation for the figures.

3. MOLD THE CHILDREN in the 10-year-old child People Mold. Follow directions in accompanying booklet. Mold head and upper body only. When two halves of figure are unmolded, put together and mount on a 1″ high cylinder, about 1″ in diameter. Pose in a forward-leaning position.

To make baskets of eggs boys are holding, cut a circle with large end of tube 2A, place on soft foam and press with small end of same tube. Hand model the eggs and fill the baskets, securing with egg white. To make chickens in girls' hands, hand model small and tiny gum paste balls, attach with egg white and pipe beaks and eyes with tube 1s.

Dress and complete the figures as booklet directs. Secure baskets and chickens to hands.

4. COMPLETE THE SCENE. Mound royal icing on prepared base, set a half-egg in position and place green foundation within it. Attach children's figures. Pipe a line of icing around edge of half-egg and carefully press on second half-egg.

Cut ¼″ strips of thin gum paste, brush egg white around oval openings and apply strips. Add more strips covering seam and dividing egg vertically into fourths. Edge with tube 1 scallops and dots. Cut eight green leaves with large violet cutter and arrange them in a circular fan-shape at top of egg. Attach while wet with egg white. Trim base and windows with flowers and add a few tube 65s leaves. Finish with a ribbon bow.

Easter treats to make children happy

YELLOW CHICKS are dressed in their best and pose on doughnut nests. Bring them out for Easter breakfast. Bake and fill egg cupcakes, cover with poured fondant and set each on a doughnut. Attach ribbons around seams, top with a bow and a drop flower on a wire stem. Pipe tube 4 blue eyes, tube 66 beaks and add tube 233 grass.

PINK RABBITS march around a little square cake. Sugar-mold eight rabbits and the ribbon-tied egg on the cake top and dry. Pipe drop flowers with tubes 14, 225 and 131. Bake, fill and ice an 8″ square cake. Write message on top with tube 2, place egg on cake top and pipe pink ribbon with tube 104. Use same tube for pleated top border. Attach rabbits to sides of cake with icing and give them piping gel eyes and noses. Pipe tube 233 grass and sprinkle with flowers. Serve to twelve.

YES, IT'S BUGS BUNNY! Your favorite rabbit rests on an egg-shaped cake as he chomps a carrot. Pipe a few tube 131 drop flowers. Bake, fill and ice an egg cake. Trim off base for stability on serving tray. Mark top with a 5″ plastic egg mold and drop string guidelines for scallops. Fill in entire lower part of cake with tube 16 stars. Trim with flowers and tube 67 leaves. Set Bugs Bunny on cake top and garnish with buttercream carrots piped with tube 7. Pipe curly carrot tops with tube 1. Serve to twelve.

Quick & Pretty

27

Figure pipe a frolicking lamb

There just couldn't be a sweeter Easter cake than this one! High relief figure piping creates the frisky little lamb—he gambols on a gum paste plaque to lift off and save as a souvenir of a happy occasion.

Are you a novice in the art of figure piping? This is an excellent project to start with—you'll be delighted at how easily the little figure takes form.

1. THE LAMB. Using *Celebrate! VI* pattern, cut a circle for the plaque from rolled gum paste. Dry thoroughly, then transfer pattern for lamb to plaque. Since the plaque will not be eaten, you may use tracing paper for this. Make a recipe of Figure piping icing.

2. Pressure control is the secret of successful figure piping. First pipe the lamb's left legs with tube 4, using even pressure to let the forms build up. Pipe right ear and tail with the same tube.

Change to tube 8 and pipe the body, starting at neck and moving back. Pause to let the icing build up at chest. Insert tube into body and pipe the rear leg, letting icing build up where it joins body. Do front leg the

same way, letting icing mound up for shoulder and knobby knee. Pipe the head and shell-shaped right ear. Insert tube into head and pipe rounded cheek. Make a groove in ear with a stick.

3. Cover the lamb with tiny tube 1s strokes for fur. Pipe eyes and little hooves with tube 4. Brush groove in ear with thinned icing. Tie the ribbon with tube 101s, and finish the plaque with a tube 3 beaded edge. Give a shine to the eyes by brushing with white corn syrup.

4. THE CAKE. This simple setting for the lamb features unusual and effective uses of tubes. *Drop flower tube 224* pipes the borders and *petal tube 101s* prints the message.

First pipe drop flowers with tube 225. Bake, fill and ice a two-layer 9″ x 13″ sheet cake. Mark position of plaque on cake top, transfer message pattern and pipe with tube 101s. Hold the tube flat as possible, full width touching cake. For curves, keep wide end of tube at inner edge of curve.

5. At base of cake, pipe deeply curved shells with tube 224. Use the same tube for top shell border. Set

plaque in position on dots of icing. Pipe grass with tube 2 and add a scattering of flowers. Trim base border with flowers and tube 2 green buds. Lift plaque off cake before serving to 24.

Decorator's secret. If you decorate for profit, prepare for busy days by making a number of these plaques ahead of time. They'll be ready to set on simply trimmed cakes.

Quick & Pretty Easter basket

Make a child very happy by giving him this pretty Easter treat!

1. Bake and fill a little 6″ round two-layer cake. Ice side yellow and mound green icing on top. Cover the side with tube 46 basket weaving, then pipe a tube 17 rope border at base and a tube 16 rope border at top.

2. Set colorful candy eggs on the cake top, then fill in spaces with tube 233 for grass. Add a ribbon bow and the little basket is finished. Serves six.

Showery flowery cakes for spring

Celebrate the season with spring's dainty flowers—some new and piped directly on the cake!

White violet below

A ruffled dream cake for a bride-to-be! First pipe the white violets with tubes 101 and 1. Dry, then mount a dozen or so on wire stems. Twist stems together for a bouquet and tie to a lacy plastic parasol. Attach a few violets to the inside of the parasol.

1. Bake, fill and ice a two-layer 9″ heart cake. Mark a heart shape on top, about 1¼″ in from edge. Divide each side of heart into sixths and mark about 1½″ up from base. Drop string guidelines for ruffles, starting first string drop about 1″ down from top edge at point of heart.

2. Fill area from guidelines to marked heart on cake top with tube 1s cornelli. Pipe a tube 6 bulb border at base, then pipe ruffles with tube 104. Do beading above ruffles and defining heart with tube 2. Fill triangular area at point of heart with violets and add tube 67 leaves. Serve to twelve.

Hyacinth at right

1. This showy little cube cake is really quick to trim. Bake, fill and ice a three-layer 6″ square cake and write message on cake top with tube 3. Pipe a tube 16 top shell border.

2. In exact center of sides of cake, pull up tube 10 stems, about 2½″

30

long. Using icing tinted the colors of the flowers, pipe long oval-shaped mounds above the stems with tube 10. Cover the mounds with five-petal, tube 76 flowers, pulling out from centers. Add a few more single petals to fill out. Stiffen the icing and pull up tube 401 leaves, holding one pointed edge of tube against cake. Finish by piping a tube 17 zigzag border. Serves ten.

Tulip time below

The most spring-like cake of all is graced with brilliant tulips, piped right on the cake.

To make the bouquet of miniature tulips, first insert a length of florist's wire into a cone fitted with tube 6 and pull out a pointed bulb. With tube 79, pull up three evenly spaced petals from base of bulb, then add three more petals between them. Pipe long tube 66 leaves on wire (page 113). Dry, then arrange in a little plastic watering can.

1. Bake, fill and ice a two-layer 8" cake. Make a pattern from a 6" paper circle, folded in sixths, for the scallops and mark on cake top. Divide base of cake in sixths.

2. Pipe six groups of tube 5 stems on side of cake. At ends of stems, pull up a tube 401 petal, curved side of tube against cake. Pipe an oval mound on top of petal, then add three more overlapping petals to cover mound. Add long tube 70 leaves, *holding one side of tube against cake.*

3. Pipe tube 104 pleated borders at base and top of cake. Pipe inner scallops with tube 76, frame with tube 3 string and add tube 13 rosettes. Set bouquet on cake and serve to ten.

Fanciful flowery eggs

MAKE EASTER HAPPIER

First mold the eggs

1. In a bowl, knead two egg whites into five pounds of granulated sugar until mixture is evenly moist. Divide into several portions and tint by kneading in liquid food color.

2. Pack the moist sugar into 5″ two-piece plastic egg molds. Level the top with a spatula, place a cake circle on the mold, invert and lift off mold. With a taut thread, trim about ½″ off the base of the molds for upright eggs. Mark "windows" on the molds with a 3″ mold.

3. Dry about two hours, then gently hold a half-egg in your palm and scoop out the moist sugar from the inside with a teaspoon, leaving ¼″ wall. Carve out windows with a small sharp knife and dry thoroughly.

Decorator's secret. The egg white mixture makes a specially strong mold that will last for years. For a touch of sparkle, knead edible glitter into the sugar mixture. We like to make large windows so the decorations are visible.

A duckling family

Mold the two halves in the top part of the 5″ egg mold, trim off base, hollow out and carve windows. Mound green royal icing in the center of a 5½″ separator plate and set a half-egg on it. Set five or six plastic ducklings on the icing and pipe grass with tube 233. Pipe a line of icing around edge of half-egg and press second half-egg against it. Cover seam and edge windows by attaching tubes 35 and 26 drop flowers. Secure mother duck to plate and add more flowers and tube 65 leaves.

Violet bouquet egg

Mold in 5″ egg mold, trim off base and cut window in one side.

1. Pipe royal icing violets with tube 101 petals, tube 1 centers. Mount on wire stems (page 113) and pipe tube 66 leaves on wires. Form bouquet. Pipe icing into a 2½″ bell mold and set bouquet in it.

Make two wings of butterfly using

Color Flow technique and *Celebrate! VI* pattern. Use tube 1 for outlining and trim. Lay a fine, uncovered wire on wax paper and pipe a tube 3 body on its end. Add artificial stamens for antennae, insert wings into body and prop to dry.

2. Mound icing on top of a Decorator Base. Set rear half-egg on it, then set bell with bouquet inside. Pipe icing around edge of half-egg and press windowed front of egg against it. Cover seam with ribbon. Pipe a tube 103 ruffle around window and finish with tube 2 beading. Arrange a few violets within opening of base and add a bow. Edge ribbon with tube 1 dots, then secure a few violets, the butterfly and a bow at top of egg.

Yellow candy box egg

This frilly box holds chocolates! Use 5″ mold and hollow out.

1. Pipe royal icing lilies with tube 66 and add tube 3 centers. Pipe daffodils with tube 103 petals and tube 2 center cups. Pipe forget-me-nots with tube 101. Cut two strips of tulle, 1½″ wide and a yard long and gather.

2. Mound icing in center of a 5½″ separator plate, arrange a circle of ruffled tulle on it, stretch an 18″ length of ribbon across it, then set base of egg on ribbon. Trim with tube 2.

Mark an oval on top half of egg mold with a 3″ mold. Trim mold with tube 2. Fill base of egg with candy then cover with top half-egg. Bring up ribbon from base, securing with icing. Pipe a line of icing around marked oval and secure ruffle to it. Edge with tube 3 beading. Pipe dots on ruffles, arrange flowers and bow. To open box, snip ribbon.

Blossom eggs

These pretty eggs are molded from summer coating in 3″ molds, each about 3 ounces. Follow directions for melting on page 146, fill molds, chill and unmold. Secure halves with melted coating. Pipe fine line borders (see page 8) with tube 1s, then add lilies, daffodils and apple blossoms.

Quick & Pretty Cakes

FOR ST. PATRICK'S DAY...THE GRANDEST CELEBRATION OF ALL!

TRIM THE CAKE with tints of emerald. Set out the shamrocks, boil the cabbage and corned beef! Put on the green and have a roaring good time!

Erin go bragh!

Ireland forever! Letter this noble battle cry of ancient Irish warriors on a sheet cake and adorn it with a big green shamrock. This cake won't take long at all so you'll have plenty of time for the party.

1. Bake, fill and ice a two-layer 9″ x 13″ sheet cake. Cover three heart-shaped cupcakes with poured fondant and place in shamrock formation on the top. Add a tube 6 stem and tube 3 beading. Use tube 3 again for lettering (use *Celebrate! VI* pattern, if you like).

2. Pipe a tube 10 bulb border at base, tube 8 border at top edge. Sprinkle a few shamrocks on the cake sides by piping heart shapes with tube 6 bulbs. Add tube 3 stems. Serve to 27, the green hearts going to the wee folk.

Smiling Irish eyes

Did you know that "Irish Eyes" is the name of a chrysanthemum? Better plant some in your garden—they're just as pretty as the song.

1. Pipe petals for the two sizes of "Irish Eyes" with tubes 104 and 103

and boiled icing. Add tube 5 green centers and dry.

2. Bake, fill and ice a two-layer 9″ x 13″ sheet cake. Mark a rectangle on cake top by measuring 1½″ in from each edge. Use this as a guide for piping a tube 2B frame. Pipe script with tube 2. Use tube 1D to frame the base of the cake, and add a *cross tube* 52 shell border. Use the same tube for the shell border at top of cake. Trim the frame with tiny crosses piped with tube 50, then attach flowers to frame and to base corners. Serves 24 merry-makers.

A sweetheart of a cake

Decorate this little cake for the sweetest colleen you know!

1. Pipe mock-shamrock flowers with tubes 140 and 33 in boiled or buttercream icing, add tube 2 centers and freeze or air-dry. Pipe shamrock leaves with tube 103, by piping three heart-shaped petals on a flower nail. Dry within curved surface.

2. Bake, fill and ice a two-layer 9″ heart cake, Mark a heart on top of cake about 1½″ in from edges. Use piping gel and tube 1s for the script. Pipe a reverse shell border at base with tube 19, a tube 16 top shell border. Using marked heart as guide, attach leaves and flowers with icing. Add a cluster of leaves and flowers at base of cake. Serve to twelve.

A cake for a baby shower or for a christening is such fun to decorate, and makes the new parents very happy!

Baby in a basket...a charming challenge

Won't the new mother be thrilled when she sees this cute little baby figure sitting in a bassinet? This sweet ornament is made of gum paste to treasure as a lasting souvenir of the party.

1. Make the basket first. Using *Celebrate! VI* pattern, cut oval shape from a 2½″ thick block of styrofoam. Taper the oval with a sharp knife so base is a little smaller than top. Ice with royal icing. Roll out a strip of gum paste about 16″ x 2½″. Roll a ridged rolling pin lightly over it to give texture. Paint the basket with egg white and wrap the strip smoothly around it, trimming and butting seam at back. Trim off neatly at top and bottom. For bassinet cover, follow pattern to cut an oval from rolled gum paste and ruffle edges by rolling with a modeling stick. Secure to top of bassinet with egg white. Cut a 3¼″ square from rolled gum paste for blanket. Mark decorative edges with a marking wheel and drape over bassinet, first painting the cover with egg white. Add tube 1s embroidery to one corner.

Cut out flowers from thinly rolled gum paste using forget-me-not and violet cutters. Place cut flowers on soft foam and press centers with a modeling stick to curve. Add tube 1 centers and dry.

2. The five-year-old People Mold is used for the baby figure. Read the instruction book for general directions. Mold head and upper torso only. While still wet, push down the head to shorten neck and trim off bottom sides of torso to a "V" shape. Dry. For legs, roll flesh-colored gum paste to a cylinder about 1½″ long x ½″. Bend ends up for feet and cut top at an angle. Curve for knee and attach to torso with gum paste. Dry. For

dress, cut a 1½″ x 4″ strip from thinly rolled gum paste, roll one edge with a modeling stick to ruffle, paint upper torso with egg white and wrap around figure. Smooth to shoulders, trim and butt seam in back.

Hand-model arms from 1¼″ x ⅜″ cylinders. Make tiny cuts for fingers, curve and attach to shoulders with egg white.

Ruffle narrow strips of gum paste and secure to shoulders for sleeves. When figure is dry, "make up" the face and use tube 1s and royal icing to pipe hair, dress trim and booties. Secure figure to bassinet with icing and add ribbon bows.

3. The cake is a sweetly simple stage. Bake, fill and ice a two-layer 10″ square cake. Pipe message with tube 2. Do base and top shell borders with tube 17. Pipe the ruffled garlands very quickly with *star-cut tube* 87. Add tube 17 upright shells at points. Pipe bows and string above garlands with tube 2. Place an oval of plastic wrap in center of cake and set bassinet baby on it. Secure flowers with icing. Serve to 20 party guests.

Flower-filled booties... Quick & Pretty delight

1. Pipe tubes 193 and 35 royal icing drop flowers and mount on wire stems. Pipe tube 66 leaves on wires. (See page 113.) When dry, twist stems together into two bouquets. Lace a pair of Crystal Clear Booties with ribbon and insert bouquets. Secure booties to a 5½″ separator plate (from Mini-tier set) with royal icing and add a little card, lettered with thinned food color.

2. Now just bake and fill a two-layer 10″ round cake. Swirl with boiled icing and pipe the curvy shell border with tube 508. Set your pretty ornament on top and present it to the mother-to-be before serving the cake to 14.

Almost as sweet as baby!

Ruffles ring a flower-shaped cake

Here's a cake just as sunny as a baby's first smile! The fluffy ruffles are accented with dainty posies piped right on the cake. There's a little lesson in lettering on this cake, too.

1. Bake and fill a two-layer 12″ petal cake and bake a single-layer 6″ round tier. Ice and assemble.

2. Make a pattern for the top tier. Fold a 5½″ paper circle in eighths, then cut a curve at the open end. Open up to reveal a petal shape to guide ruffles. With a compass, draw a 4½″, then a 4″ circle on the pattern. Within the space defined by the circles print your message. Make sure that all vertical strokes in the letters radiate from the center of the pattern. Do this by holding a ruler from the center to the outer marked circle. Transfer pattern to tier, then pipe message with tube 2.

3. Pipe a tube 18 shell border at base of petal cake, a tube 16 shell border at top. Edge upper tier with tube 16 shells at base, tube 15 shells at top.

Drop string guidelines for ruffles at base of petal cake and pipe ruffles with tube 125. Use the same tube for triple ruffles on top, following curve of cake, and from outer edge in. Pipe tube 104 ruffles on top tier.

4. Pipe the pretty flowers. Pipe a tube 2 dot to mark center of flower, then pull out five petals with *star-cut tube* 75. Hold the tube with the two longest teeth up. Fill centers with tube 2 stamens, then pipe tube 65 leaves. Set a little candy-filled bassinet on the cake top and serve to 30 guests.

Decorator's secret. Careful planning and accurate piping can turn a simple cake into a work of art.

Cherubs tell good news

1. Pipe pastel drop flowers in royal icing with tubes 191, 225, 177 and 106. Add tube 1 centers and dry. Bake and fill a two-layer 9" x 13" sheet cake and bake a heart cup cake. Ice and assemble. Pipe message on cupcake with tube 1. Pipe tube 1 cornelli on sides of cupcake, then add tube 1 beading at top, tube 3 beading at base.

Measure 3" in from each corner on sides of sheet cake and mark about 1½" up from base. Divide remaining space on long sides into thirds.

2. Pipe tube 17 shell borders at bottom and top of sheet cake. Now use the same tube to pipe zigzag curved garlands on sides. Top with tube 104 swags and tube 17 rosettes.

3. Place Angel Musicians on cake top. Mark curves above and below heart, cover with a tube 17 zigzag garland, then cover garland with flowers. Attach two Angelinos to each corner of cake at sides with icing, then arrange flowers below them on dots of icing. Serves 24.

Decorator's secret. Either of these two cakes would serve just as nicely for a bridal announcement or shower. Just change the messages, and replace the bassinet with a cupid.

Good luck, graduates

Celebrate their "coming out" with symbols of wisdom attained (the owls), enduring friendship (the ivy) and departure (sweet peas).

1. Figure pipe the owls on wax paper in advance in the upright, three-dimensional method. Use figure piping icing (page 157). Hold tube 1A straight up, apply heavy pressure and pipe the oval body. Lift tube as icing builds up until body is about 2" tall, stop pressure, then move away. Let icing set up a little, then add a tube 1A ball for head.

When owls are almost dry, pipe tube 2 horns and beaks. Pipe wing feathers with tube 101, then cover owls with short strokes of tube 1. Pipe tube 28 "star" eyes, then top with tube 4 dots. Dry completely.

2. Pipe ruffled sweet peas with tube 103. Do graduation year in Color Flow, using Celebrate! VI pattern and outlining with tube 3. Fill in and dry on 14" curve.

3. Bake, ice and assemble a two-layer 14" round cake and a cake in the horseshoe pan. Print "good luck" on the horseshoe cake. Pipe tube 18 fleurs-de-lis at base of 14" cake, then add a tube 17 star border. At top of cake, pipe a tube 17 shell border.

4. Pipe a tube 16 shell border at base of horseshoe, a tube 15 border at top. Mark a curve on top and side of 14" cake and attach flowers. Trim with tube 66 ivy—piped as triple leaves. Pipe ivy on top of horseshoe and set owls in position. Pipe tube 2 claws. Secure Color Flow number to front of cake. Horseshoe serves twelve, round cake 36.

Good luck...to the graduates

40

Good luck, co-worker

Deck the cake with sunny coreopsis, the flower of cheerfulness, and ivy vines for faithful friendship. The little plastic figure shows his favorite occupation in the years ahead!

1. Pipe the new flowers with royal icing, tube 104 and a number 7 nail. Move the tube back and forth from center of nail to edge, to form each of the eight notched petals. Lift tube up as you finish the petal to give it fluff—then start the next petal. Fill center with tube 1 dots, then slide off nail to dry within curve. Mount some of the flowers on wire stems (page 113) and pipe triple tube 67 leaves on wire. Form a bouquet with stemmed flowers and leaves.

2. Bake and ice a horseshoe cake and set it on a two-layer 12" x 18" iced cake. This big cake will serve a crowd! Pipe message on horseshoe. Pipe a double curved vine with *multiple hole tube 43* on side of sheet cake, then add short stems with tube 3. Pipe a curved shell base border with tube 19, a top shell border with tube 17.

3. On horseshoe cake drop double strings with one motion of *time-saving tube 43*. Add zigzag top and corner borders with the same tube. Finish with a tube 17 shell border at base. Set bouquet on cake and add more flower trim. Pipe ivy leaves as three leaves with tube 67—first a leaf in center, then one on either side. Complete with a Frustrated Fisherman figure (or choose the figure that best expresses his favorite sport). Sheet cake serves 54, horseshoe serves twelve. Give the bouquet and figure to the honored guest as souvenirs of a happy party.

...to the happy retiree

For your favorite girl!

In Japan, each year on March 3, a charming celebration is held called "girls' day." Girls' day is part of the springtime Peach Blossom Festival. In each home fortunate enough to have a girl, elaborately dressed dolls representing the emperor and empress and their court are brought out and arranged on a red-draped background. Sprays of peach blossoms decorate the display. The little girls then hold tea parties in front of the scene.

Translate this pretty custom and have a party for your favorite girl.

1. Pipe the five-petaled peach blossoms with tube 102 and fill the centers with tube 1s stamens. Pipe smaller blossoms with tubes 101 and 101s. Bake and ice a single-layer 10″ round cake and bake a cake in the Wonder Mold. Ice a marshmallow to the top of the Wonder Mold cake and insert doll pick. Ice the cake, filling in around marshmallow, and assemble with round cake. Mark curves on skirt.

2. Fill in triangular area at hem with tube 16 stars. Pipe the double ruffle with three petal tubes, 124, 104 and 103 to give the tapered effect. Fill in rest of skirt with tube 16 stars.

Mound icing at top of arms for puffed sleeves, then cover bodice and sleeves with tube 13 stars. Pipe neck and sleeve ruffles with tube 102. "Print" the dress with tube 23.

3. Pipe a tube 16 shell border at base of round cake, a tube 13 border at top. Drop tube 13 strings and finish with rosettes. Attach the ring of flowers and pipe tube 65 leaves.

Wire the doll's wrists together and fasten a ribbon bow to the wire. Add tiny peach blossoms and trim with 65s leaves. Serve to 20 girls.

Decorator's secret. The marshmallow on top of the Wonder Mold makes the skirt longer and more graceful.

Celebrate!®

MAY AND JUNE

Gloria and Jim

Directions for this Australian engagement cake, page 52

43

Wedding Cakes...they're wonderful!

FOR ME, and I think for every decorator, the wedding cake is the ultimate decorated cake. It's important for the bride—a beautiful cake is the crown of the happiest day of her life. It's important for the decorator. The tiers of a towering bridal cake give a wonderful opportunity to use and display the skill and artistry that result in a real masterpiece.

A wedding cake really expresses the personality of a decorator, too. As you gain experience, and decorate more and more bridal cakes, you'll find that each one is more satisfying to do than the last, and expresses more of your own taste.

THE FIVE CAKES shown on the following pages pretty well sum up my ideas on decorating wedding cakes. Perhaps they'll be of help to you when you start on the exciting task of trimming your next tier cake.

What is the most important element in a wedding cake?

What makes one cake different than another, even at a glance, and perhaps makes it more beautiful, too? *It's the proportion of the entire cake itself.*

First of all, I'm taking it for granted that the tiers are baked and put together properly. The article starting on page 16 is a good refresher.

BEFORE YOU EVEN BEGIN to bake, think of the cake as a unit. Indeed, think of it as a piece of architecture made up of tiers of various sizes, pillars to separate the tiers, cupids and other sculptural trims, and finally the crown of the top ornament. If all the elements of this structure add up to a pleasingly proportioned unit, you will have a beautiful cake.

You may use almost any type of border, simple or elaborate, add almost any kind or color of flower, cover the tiers with rolled or poured fondant or buttercream. The structure of the cake is still the most important element in your cake's beauty.

That's why I assemble the cake completely and walk all around it to view it thoroughly before I begin to decorate. The cake itself tells me what borders and other trim to use. It will for you too.

A RULE OF THUMB is to make each tier 4″ smaller than the one below it. It's a good rule, but one you can sometimes break as the cakes that follow illustrate.

Color in wedding cakes

A wedding cake should be dainty— not bright or garish. That's why I almost always start with a white cake and then add pastel or white flowers to set it off. Of course, a delicate pastel cake with white borders and flowers is pretty, too.

EXTEND THE COLOR accents through the entire cake. In the cake at right, see how the yellow flowers are repeated on every tier. This gives a pleasing, unified effect.

Sometimes, to bring the top ornament into the scheme, I'll color-spray the white flowers on it.

A beautiful wedding cake is the sum of many details. Color is a very important part of the whole effect.

Some questions answered

WHAT ICING TO USE is asked by many of you. *Buttercream* covers most of our wedding cakes, and it's just a matter of practice to put it on smoothly. *For borders I prefer boiled icing.* (Recipe is on page 156.) It pipes out of the tube easily, has a nice glossy look and avoids that too-rich taste that a heavy buttercream border has. *For flowers, I recommend royal icing.* You can make them up far in advance and the details are sharp and perfect. People like to take home a royal icing flower as a souvenir, and most people, in these weight-conscious times, don't like to eat a heavy flower piped in buttercream. I find that boiled icing pipes a nice light flower, too, but royal icing is my first choice.

HOW MUCH BATTER to use for various sizes of pans is another frequent question. There is no firm answer to that, because recipes and cake mixes vary so much in their rising properties. You'll just have to depend on your own experience in baking.

HOW MUCH ICING is needed for various sizes of cakes depends on your own experience, too and the design of the cake. Most of the icing recipes in this book can be properly stored and rebeaten to use again. Make plenty of icing—then you won't have to worry that you will run out before the cake is finished.

PERFECT STRING WORK is a problem for some of you. Since stringwork sets off so many wedding cakes, it's wise to perfect your skill in piping it. First of all, *thin the icing* until it flows evenly out of the tube and won't break. Secondly, touch the tube to the cake and let the string drop by itself— *never* follow the curve. Then touch again. Thirdly, *work rhythmically* for evenly draped strings.

SILK FLOWERS? Yes, they're pretty on a cake, and real flowers much more lovely. But the decorator in me prefers to use piped or gum paste flowers to keep the entirely handmade, artistic look of the cake.

Yellow sweet pea

A slender tower of a cake with the top tier lifted and crowned by an arch of flowers. Directions are on page 47

Lady Windemere

A gracious traditional design
graced with golden arcs of flowers

LADY WINDEMERE gives an impression of dignified beauty. To lighten the effect, I've lifted the top tier on rather tall pillars, created an airy, lofty ornament, and used sculptured cupids to soften the design. The flowers add a lot to this cake, too.

This cake is convenient to bake, if you don't have a big oven. The largest pan size you'll need is 14" round.

1. WORK IN ADVANCE. Pipe royal icing roses and buds with tubes 124 and 104. Pipe tube 102 daisies.

Prepare the cake board by setting four 12" round pans on a sheet of corrugated cardboard. Trace around them, then draw a line 2" beyond the tracing. Cut this pattern out three times from cardboard (strength is needed for this heavy cake). Tape the boards together, cover with foil, then glue a satin ribbon around the edge.

Make the top ornament by clipping the wings from three Cherub Concerto figures. Glue them on a Heart Base, then arch artificial flowers over them. Clip wings off four more cherub figures to set on the cake board.

2. PREPARE THE TIERS, all are two-layers. The base tier is made up of four 12" cakes. Above them is a 14" tier, then an 8" tier at top. The lower tiers are 4" high, the top tier 3".

Fill and ice all the tiers, then construct them on the cake board, using a seated cherub separator set. Place the ornament on top. Lift off upper tiers and start decorating.

3. DO TOP TRIM on the four cakes that make up the base tier first. Make a paper pattern by folding a 12" circle in sixths. Cut an arc from the two folded edges, then cut a curved arch from the open end of the folded pattern. Open to reveal pointed ovals framed by arches. Transfer to cake tops. With a circular motion, outline pattern with tube 2. Replace upper tiers.

Do bottom border on base tier with tube 32 reverse shells. From top edge, drop string guidelines for garlands, using top pattern as guide.

Pipe garlands with *star-cut tube 73*, then pipe a ruffled leaf between each with same tube. Trim garlands with double tube 3 string. Pipe a puffy shell top border with tube 21. Frame the shells with tube 3 string dropped in "S" curves, below one shell, then above the next.

4. *At base of 14" tier* pipe puffy stars with tube 22, then drop tube 3 string over them. Divide top of tier into sixteenths, using pillars as guide. Mark top with a cookie cutter for scallops. Drop string guidelines for garlands, using scallops as guide. Pipe garlands with tube 17, then drop strings below them with tube 4. Add a *star cut tube 73* leaf between each garland, then drop double tube 3 strings over garlands. Pipe scallops and edge separator plate with tube 4 in a circular motion. Finish with a tube 17 reverse shell top border.

5. *On top tier* pipe tube 21 inverted shells at base. Trim with double strings. Drop a tube 3 string from top of one shell, skip one and touch tube to top of third shell. Continue for interwoven look. Drop strings from top edge, first a long drop, then a short. Go back and circle the tier again with the same method. Pipe tube 16 stars for top border. *Please note:* for tiny string drops like these, you must *thin the icing more*.

6. *Add flower trims.* Circle the ornament base with flowers. Set a Frolicking Cherub within pillars, heap roses around it, then add roses and daisies around seated cherubs. Form arcs of flowers on lower tier, set cherub figures on cake board, and trim with flowers. Pipe tube 65 leaves. Serve two lower tiers of beautiful Lady Windemere to 364, top tier to 30.

Yellow sweet pea page 45

Here is an elegant little example of using tiers in unusual proportions.

1. *In advance,* pipe yellow royal icing sweet peas and white tube 33 drop flowers. Dress up a Petite Heavenly Bells ornament by adding an arch of artificial flowers.

2. *Prepare the two-layer tiers.* Base tier is 12" x 4," middle tier 10" x 4," top tier 6" x 3." Fill and ice all tiers. Assemble on cake board with 6" plates and 5" Grecian pillars. Set an Angel Fountain within pillars, four Mediterranean Cupids on middle tier and the ornament on top, so you can judge final effect. Remove ornament and cupids, start decorating.

3. *Divide top edge of bottom tier* into sixteenths. Mark top of tier with cookie cutter for scallops. About 1½" down from top edge, make second marks for lower garlands. On this tier, work from top to bottom. Pipe tube 16 upper garlands from mark to mark. Trim with double tube 3 strings. From lower marks, pipe a second series of tube 16 garlands. Drop a tube 16 string over garlands, top with a tube 3 string, then pipe *star cut tube 72* leaves with very light pressure. Finish with tube 3 bows and string.

Pipe dots on cake board to define bottom border. Pipe tube 18 garlands and frame with a tube 16 dropped string. Pipe a *star cut tube 72* ruffled leaf between every other garland. Pipe tube 16 reverse shell top border.

4. *On middle tier* pipe a tube 14 reverse shell base border. Divide top edge of tier into twelfths. Mark scallops on top of tier with a cutter. Drop string guidelines and pipe garlands with tube 14, starting and ending with a curl. Drop tube 3 string below garlands, then add *tube 72* ruffled leaves. Pipe tube 3 zigzags over scallops and around plate.

5. *On top tier,* divide in twelfths and mark about ½" up from base. Drop tube 3 string from mark to mark, then pipe tube 14 "e" motion garlands over string. Cover with tube 14 curves. Add tube 72 leaves. Pipe tube 14 reverse shell top border.

Finish the cake with cascades and clusters of sweet peas. Add tube 65 leaves. Attach drop flowers to the pillars. Yellow Sweet Pea serves 116 guests from the two lower tiers. Top tier serves 16.

Pink rose

Six pillars beneath a hexagonal tier give the effect of a little temple. Directions, page 50

Daisy

Repeated curves and fragile
flowers create a very feminine
cake. Directions, page 50

Pink rose page 48

THE CONSTRUCTION of Pink Rose consists of four tiers for a graceful, lofty effect. Three two-layer round tiers—16″ 12″ and 6″—are made more dramatic by placing a 9″ hexagon tier below the top tier. Six 6½″ Arched Pillars give added height.

To give a more ornate look to the pillars, I glued an Angelino to the top of each. I chose a petite Spring Song top ornament, then trimmed it with a few pink drop flowers. I trimmed the little cherub within the pillars with flowers, too. This carries the color up the cake and gives a more individual, finished look to the whole cake.

Try adding your own touches to the pillars and ornaments you use on your wedding cakes. You'll create a really unique cake for the bride.

THE FLOWERS. Roses are a favorite for wedding cakes, but, of course, you could use any type or color of flower the bride wishes. For the base and hexagon tiers, I put the roses in formal, symmetrical arrangements, but for the other two tiers I piped dainty sprays of rosebuds and drop flowers to give a lighter effect. I even piped a little flowering vine on the pillars. (*Note:* thin the icing with corn syrup to make it stick to the plastic surface.)

THE BORDERS on Pink Rose are very traditional. To make a "hanging border" like that on the hexagon tier, drop string curves, starting about ½″ up from the base of the tier. Cover the string with a zigzag or circular motion garland. I added a ruffled tube 72 leaf between each garland. Be sure to thin the icing when you pipe leaves so they'll draw out to nice points.

Pink Rose serves 208, with the top tier saved for the first anniversary.

Daisy page 49

THE CONSTRUCTION of this cake is classic—four round tiers, 16″, 12″ 10″ and 6″ To give it a lift, I put a flyaway lovebird ornament on top and raised the two upper tiers on 5″ pillars. The four little cupids which are set near the pillars soften the construction, too, and so does the "hanging border" on the 10″ tier.

I CHOSE DAISIES to trim this cake because of their airy, fluffy look. Just the little golden centers warm up the all-white cake. Notice how the flowers gradually decrease in size as the tiers get smaller.

There's a real art in arranging flowers in a graceful, natural way. Pipe a little mound of icing on the cake, then set the flower on it, tilting it this way or that so it looks its best to the viewer. Drying the flowers in a curved form gives them a nice, natural look, too.

THE BORDERS on Daisy are really a variation on a garland theme. The "hanging border" on the 10″ tier is done in a similar way to the one on Pink Rose. The three lower tiers of Daisy serve 234, the top tier 16.

White Rose at right

UNUSUAL CONSTRUCTION makes White Rose a very impressive cake. The focal point is the 14″ square base tier, designed to be viewed from the front corner. Above it are four 7½″ high pillars, then 12″ and 8″ round tiers. To make the cake really outstanding, I designed a new top ornament. Glue two cherub figures back-to-back on a heart ornament base, then add an arch of flowers. The base tier is big enough to carry four rather large cherub figures.

FLOWERS are an important design element in this cake. The four curves of roses on the base tier accent the square shape. I covered a half-ball of styrofoam with roses and set it within the pillars. The top tier I left very simple to set off the flower cascades.

BORDERS are heavy and lavish. Each of the two lower tiers has a triple garland trim. I trimmed the pillars with royal icing hearts dried on a curve, then covered them with drop flowers after they were attached to the pillars. Just a few soft green leaves set off the flowers. The top tier serves 30, the two lower tiers 166.

White rose

Very Victorian with
contrasting shapes of tiers
and lavish trim

HOW THE EXPERTS DO IT: HOA DONG

A bridal shower cake in the Australian Style

Of all the foreign methods of decorating, the Australian style is the most unmistakeable, and perhaps the most beautiful. Important hallmarks are perfect proportion, delicate embroidery, fragile lace and the daintiest of curtaining. These elements combine for a look of refined simplicity. Here, Hoa Dong shows you step-by-step how to create the lovely shower cake on page 43. It's so beautiful it could serve as a petite wedding cake.

Make flowers and pipe lace pieces

The flowers on the prettiest Australian cakes are made of gum paste. Use the recipe on page 158. To make two roses and leaves, use the small rose and rose leaf cutters from the Flower Garden set, and follow directions that come with the cutters. For the stephanoti use the metal stephanotis cutter. You will need four or five. Form a base from a small piece of gum paste by modeling it into a cone about ⅜″ high. Make a tiny hook in one end of a length of florists' wire, dip in egg white and insert in cone. Stick wire in styrofoam to dry. Roll out gum paste thin as possible, cut flower shape and lay on a thin sheet of foam. Press each petal from center to tip with the round end of modeling stick. Dip prepared base in egg white and fold flower shape around it. Brush a little egg white on edges of flower to join. Smooth onto wire stem. Curve petals outward and dry. Twist stems of one rose, stephanoti and leaves together to form a bouquet and tie with ribbon.

Pipe lace pieces with egg white royal icing. Tape *Celebrate! VI* patterns to a stiff surface, tape wax paper over them and pipe with tube 1s.

Prepare the cake and cover with rolled fondant

Australian cakes are covered with rolled fondant for a satin-smooth decorating surface. With a little practice, this is easy to do—students have learned to cover a cake in ten minutes! Recipes are on page 157.

1. Bake a two-layer pound or fruit cake in 9″ heart pans. Layers should be about 1½″ high. Fill layers with apricot jam, and attach cake to a cardboard base, same size and shape. Make a recipe of marzipan and one of rolled fondant. Fill any crevices or holes in the cake by packing in bits of marzipan. Brush hot apricot glaze over entire surface of cake. (Heat one cup of apricot jam to boiling and strain.)

2. Dust work surface and rolling pin with confectioners' sugar, then roll out marzipan about ¼″ thick to a circle about 16″ in diameter. Fold marzipan over rolling pin, place on top edge of cake and unroll over cake. Smooth marzipan over entire cake by gently pressing with your hands. If a crack appears, pinch it together and smooth again. Trim off edges at base. Brush again with apricot glaze.

3. Now coat your work surface and rolling pin with non-stick pan release, dust with cornstarch and roll out a fondant circle about ¼″ thick and 16″ in diameter. Place fondant circle over cake, then smooth into place with your hands. Fondant is elastic so this will be easy. Trim off base, smooth again with your hands and trim again. With a few strokes of corn syrup, secure cake to a foil-covered board, cut 1½″ larger than cake all around. You may cover the cake several days ahead of decorating time, as the covering seals in the moisture.

Pipe the dainty trim

1. Using cake pan as guide, make a 6″ heart pattern and mark a 5″ heart within it. Transfer to cake top, then write message with tube 1s and a mixture of half royal icing, half piping gel. Transfer pattern for curtaining to cake sides, lowest point about ⅜″ above base. Mark pattern at point of heart first, then on sides, skipping one space to allow room for ribbon. Curtaining will not meet at back of heart at indentation. Attach ribbon from inner heart to base of cake with dots of icing. Use egg white royal icing for all decorating, *sieving sugar three times* to be sure it is lump-free. Pipe a tube 4 bulb border at base of cake.

2. Fill the marked heart with tube 000 cornelli lace, then edge heart and ribbon with a "snail's trail" (bulb border) and tiny scallops. Pipe the embroidery at top edge and sides of cake freehand with the same tube.

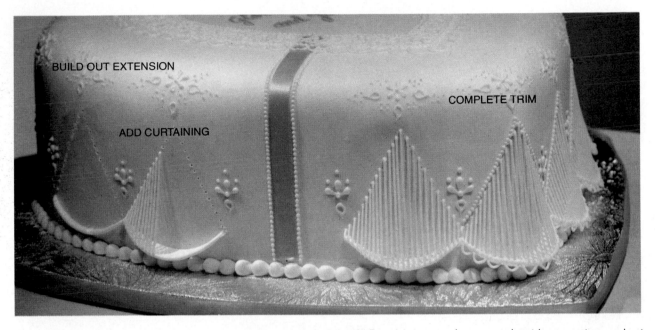

BUILD OUT EXTENSION

ADD CURTAINING

COMPLETE TRIM

3. Now for the curtaining! Pipe scalloped extension to support it with tube 1. First pipe a line the full width of the base of each triangle, then a second, shorter line on top and in the center of it. Repeat four more times, making a total of six lines, each line shorter than the one preceding it. After piping two lines, pause to let the icing dry. Finally pipe a finishing line around each little "shelf." Brush surface with thinned icing to smooth. Dry. Complete the curtaining with tube 000. Drop strings from top of triangles to extensions, keeping spaces perfectly even. Dry thoroughly, then edge with "snail's trails" and tiny dropped strings.

4. Attach lace pieces to heart with dots of icing. Add a ribbon bow at base, and set bouquet on cake top. The curtaining does not meet at back of cake where heart indents, so place second gum paste rose there. Serve wedding cake-size pieces to 28.

Decorator's secret. For full information about the Australian method, and a group of dainty cakes, read Chapter Six, *The Wilton Way of Cake Decorating, Volume II.*

A DAINTY FAVOR for each lady is a charming custom in the Philippines. To make this one, mold two gum paste hearts using the mold in the Popular Request sugar molds. Fill one heart with sugared almonds or candy, attach second heart with royal icing and letter the initials of the honored couple with thinned food color. Trim with a ribbon loop and gum paste blossoms. Set at the guest's place.

Pearl... An anniversary cake in the English over-piped style

A gift of pearls is appropriate for the thirtieth wedding anniversary and there could be no more impressive centerpiece for the celebration than this cake in the English over-piped style. Michael Nitzsche has designed and decorated this masterpiece and shows you step-by-step how to re-create it.

The over-piped style is distinguished by line-upon-line of curving accurate piping that results in a formal, ornate, very sculptural cake. Sometimes called the Lambeth style after its best-known practitioner, this style was perfected by many skilled English decorators in the nineteenth and present century.

Preparing the cake

English over-piped cakes have an unusually lofty proportion. The cake is a fruit cake, covered first with marzipan, then royal icing for a perfectly smooth surface.

1. Bake sufficient layers of fruit cake in 10″ round pans to achieve a final height of 6.″ We baked two layers, each about 2½″ high. Brush one layer with apricot glaze (page 16), fill with a circle of marzipan, brush marzipan with glaze, then add second layer. Make sure that top of cake is completely level. Attach a cardboard cake circle, same size as the cake, to its top with royal icing. Fill in any cracks or holes by pressing in bits of marzipan.

2. Roll out a ball of marzipan to a circle about ⅜″ thick and a little larger than the diameter of cake. Brush the top of the cake (this was the bottom) with hot apricot glaze and place cake on marzipan circle, glazed side down. Press gently, then cut off excess marzipan with a sharp knife.

3. Form a long cylinder from marzipan and roll out to a width slightly larger than height of cake. With a ruler and a sharp knife straighten one long edge. Turn cake upright, brush side with apricot glaze, set cake on its side on the marzipan strip, bottom touching straight edge of marzipan, and roll it like a wheel to cover side, patting into place. Butt seam smoothly, then trim off excess marzipan on top edge. Pat entire cake to smooth, then let harden 48 hours. Cover smoothly with royal icing, dry, then cover with a second coat. Set cake on a foil-covered hexagon cake board, measuring 16″ from point to opposite point.

Decorate the top

Here directions for top and side trim are given separately, but you will find yourself working on both almost simultaneously, as you allow piped lines to crust. *Remember, complete no more than two lines of piping before allowing icing to harden.* All trim is piped in royal icing.

Please turn the page

Transfer all *Celebrate! VI* patterns to cake, lining up as picture shows. Design your own initials to fit inside top plaque, then do plaque in the "run-in" (Color Flow) method. After drying, outline edge with tube 2, then outline the letters with tube 1. Over-pipe with a second tube 1 line and edge with tube 1 dots.

1. Pipe plaque supports with four superimposed lines of tube 2. Now for the dramatic over-piping! Accuracy and a steady hand are essential. First outline outer edge of diamonds with tube 2. Over-pipe four times with the same tube, then add two pipings with tube 1. Within diamond pipe a second smaller and higher one, first with six lines of tube 2, then with two tube 1 lines. Pipe a third tiny diamond with seven lines of tube 2, and two lines of tube 1.

Pipe inner scallops and frame outer sides of diamonds with five over-piped tube 2 lines and two tube 1 lines. Move out and over-pipe four tube 2 lines and one tube 1 line. Move out again and pipe a tube 3 line over-piped with tubes 2 and 1. Pipe a fourth outline with tube 2, then tube 1,

and finally pipe a tube 1 line to complete design. Edge curves and top corners with tube 1 dots. Add large "pearls" with tube 4.

2. For upstanding curves on top edge, use only tube 2. Pipe 15 short, evenly spaced lines. Starting with second line, and ending with the next-to-the-last line, over-pipe each. Continue in this fashion until center line is over-piped seven times.

Frame the design with curved scrolls. First pipe them with zigzags done with tube 13. Over-pipe with a tube 13 line, then over-pipe with tubes 4, 3 and 2. Add curves of tube 2 "pearls" and a large pearl, where scrolls join, with tube 4. Between side designs pipe a large tube 4 pearl and trim with tube 2 curves and dots.

Decorate the side and base

1. Outline curved side scrolls with tube 1. Pipe inner curves with tube 3, over-pipe with tube 1. Edge with tube 1 dots. Outline diamond shapes with tube 3, over-pipe with two lines of tube 1. Pipe second diamond within first with tube 3, over-pipe with tube 3 and two lines of tube 1. Pipe smallest diamond with tubes 3, 3, 3, 2, 2 and 1. Pipe tube 2 pearls, bulbs and curves.

2. For base trim, start with a large tube 7 pearl. Pipe a tube 3 heart on top of it. Do curved scrolls with tube 13 zigzags, over-pipe with a tube 13 line, then with tubes 3, 3, 2 and 2. Add a fan of tube 2 bulbs at top center of design, pipe tube 2 dots above side curves, then tube 1 scallops.

In center of design at base, pipe a tube 7 pearl with a tube 3 pearl on each side. Frame pearls at base with tube 4 over-piped with tubes 3 and 2, then frame a second time with tube 3 over-piped with tube 2. Finish with tube 2 pearls and tiny tube 1 strings on cake board. Over-pipe hearts with tubes 2 and 1. Pipe dots of icing on plaque supports and position plaque. Serve your beautiful over-piped masterpiece to 36, cutting fan-fashion.

Decorator's secret. For other magnificent English over-piped cakes, and cakes decorated in the other foreign methods, read *The Wilton Way of Cake Decorating, Volume Two.*

Transfer patterns you plan to use again to stencil paper (available at art supply stores). They'll be grease-proof, waterproof and very durable.

Pink perfection

...an easy-to-decorate bridal cake. Garlands of rosy drop flowers, intriguing borders and simple stacked construction combine to make a sweet and very impressive, petite cake.

1. First make sugar mold hearts in candy molds. Pipe drop flowers with tubes 96, 33 and 225. Dry.

2. Bake, fill and ice the tiers. Base tier is two 12" round layers above a 16" base bevel. Middle tier is a two-layer 8" round. The little top tier is a single-layer 6" heart. Assemble on cake board. Divide bottom tier at bevel into twelfths, and drop string guide lines for garlands. Divide middle tier into twelfths at base, then make a second series of marks midway between the first, 2" up from base.

3. Pipe a tube 502 shell border at base of cake, a tube 501 border at top of bevel. Pipe zigzag garlands from mark to mark on bevel. About 1" below tier top, drop triple tube 2 strings, using garlands as guides. Add bows and streamers, then pipe a tube 502 reverse shell top border.

4. On middle tier, pipe zigzag garlands at base from mark to mark with tube 14, then over-pipe with a second, slightly smaller garland. Attach sugar hearts above each garland with icing. Drop a fan of tube 1 strings over hearts from marks, then edge top with tube 502 reverse shells. Pipe tube 501 shells at base of heart tier, reverse shells at top.

5. Set a petite bridal couple on top of cake and border with tube 14 shells. Now trim the cake with flowers, covering garlands on base bevel. Pipe leaves with tube 349 and set Pink Perfection on the reception table. Two lower tiers serve 98, top tier, six.

Decorator's secret. Mold ice cream in heart cupcake pans and trim with drop flowers to complete a dessert service. Return to freezer.

White birch

Above the lowest tier, slender white birch trees lift their branches to encircle a splashing fountain. You can create this enchanting woodland scene for the most talked-about wedding cake of the year!

Prepare the separators

1. *For the upper separator,* use two 14" plates (from the Crystal Clear set) and six 6½" arched pillars. Remove two pillar projections from each plate, leaving two directly opposite each other. Mark an 8" circle on plate, then glue four stud plates to plate, so you achieve six equally spaced projections for pillars. Inner edges of stud plates touch marked circle. Paint the lower plate with thinned green royal icing, dry, attach petite bridal couple to center of plate, then assemble the two plates with pillars.

2. *For the lower separator,* cut six ⅝" dowel rods into 13½" lengths. Remove all pillar projections from lower plate of Arched Pillar tier set. Mark a 12" circle on plate and glue on six evenly spaced stud plates, inner edges of stud plates touching marked circle. On upper plate, mark a 12" circle and glue on six stud plates, inner edges touching circle—one between each pillar projection.

3. Remove top level of fountain. Sugar mold the "grassy bank" that conceals motor of fountain. Use a 12" round pan and a 12" top bevel pan as molds. Stack the two molds and carve an 8" hole in the center. Ice with green royal icing and rough up with a damp sponge. Mark a 15" circle on lower plate, ice within it with thinned green royal icing and set sugar mold in center. Place fountain in hole.

4. *Set dowel rods* into stud plates on lower plate. Drill three holes in each rod at an angle at front and on each side to receive "branches." Use ³⁄₁₆"

drill bit. Twist several lengths of stiff florists' wire together, insert in holes, tape to secure and spread ends of wires for branches. Cover tree trunks with vertical tube 13 lines, building up over stud plates.

Prepare the tiers

1. Pipe royal icing drop flowers with tubes 190, 131 and 33. Paint base of twin bird ornament with thinned green icing.

2. All tiers are two layers, for a finished height of 4"—*except* top tier which is 3" high. Bake, fill and ice all tiers.

Base tier: six two-layer 9" heart cakes surrounding a 6" square styrofoam dummy, same height as cakes, iced with royal icing. Each heart is placed

on its own cake board, dummy is set on a 6" cake base.

Tier above trees: 16" round

Tier above arched pillars: 12" round

Top tier: 8" round

Decorate the cake

1. Assemble three upper tiers. Divide each in twelfths. *On 16" tier* pipe a tube 18 base shell border, feathery side scrolls with tube 16, and a tube 17 reverse shell top border. Edge separator plate with tube 16.

2. *On 12" tier,* pipe a tube 17 shell border, add curved scrolls and fleurs-de-lis with tube 16, tube 13 zigzag garlands at top. Drape garlands with tube 2 string and pipe a tube 16 reverse shell top border.

3. *On top tier,* pipe a tube 14 base shell border. Do curves and upright shells on side with tube 16, and finish with a tube 16 top border.

Trim bird ornament, three upper tiers and "grassy bank" with flowers. Add tube 65 leaves. Pipe "grass" around fountain and tree trunks with tube 2.

4. *Each heart cake* is decorated separately. Pipe a tube 18 base shell border, a tube 17 top border. Add curved scrolls on top with the same tube. Spatula-stripe a decorating bag with green icing, fill with white and pipe curves on sides with tube 17. Trim cakes with flowers.

5. Assemble on the reception table. Set heart cakes in place around dummy. Position birch tree separator with fountain. Pipe leaves on the branches with a "V"-cut cone.

Drape 4" squares of white tulle casually over branches, then cover with leaves. Set upper plate with top three tiers on tree pillars, then add a few more leaves. White Birch is complete and beautiful! Top tier serves 30, all other tiers serve 354.

Flamboyant, colorful, dramatic...and dainty. That's decorating the Philippine way

The lavish cakes created by talented Philippine decorators are achieved in spite of a lack of the many aids American decorators depend on. Pillars and separator plates are unknown, so elaborate structures of plywood and dowels are crafted to support the tiers. Ready made ornaments for bridal cakes are not available, so the ingenious Philippines make their own fanciful ornaments from gum paste. Pretty plastic cupids and other trims cannot be purchased—but this does not deter the decorator. He or she simply models them in gum paste, first making the molds.

Add to all this creative inventiveness the unique Philippine piped flowers and simple but effective border work and the distinctive dramatic style has evolved.

For basic understanding of Philippine techniques, read Chapter Four in *Volume Two, The Wilton Way of Cake Decorating*. To bring you the Philippine way of working with gum paste, we invited Roberto Rebolledo, known professionally as Dexter, an outstanding Philippine decorator, to visit the *Celebrate!* decorating room and decorate several cakes.

Dexter owns a large bakery in Quezon and also teaches classes daily in decorating. The art of decorating has reached a very advanced state in the Philippines. Bakers vie with one another to have the most outstanding displays of decorated cakes in their windows. New ideas are quickly picked up and even newer ones developed.

"Dexter" cakes are greatly admired. He designs all the important ones and strives to make every cake very personal to reflect the taste of the recipients and to express important events in their lives.

THE WEDDING CAKE Dexter decorated for *Celebrate!* readers is a resplendent example of the Philippine style with emphasis on gum paste trims. The "windowed" separators conceal electric bulbs that cast a golden glow over the spectacular scene.

Much of the work was done in advance. Plywood separators are cut out, sturdy legs are added, then assembled with ½" strips of wood. Electric fixtures are wired to the structure. Six windowed panels for each tier separation are cut from rolled gum paste, then trimmed with molded gum paste flowers and finished off with stems and leaves painted on the panels with thinned food color. Cupid figures and all parts of the temple ornament are molded. Royal icing stemmed flowers form

many ribboned bouquets.

The cakes are baked in a firm butter or pound cake recipe. Their shapes are cut from sheet cakes since shaped pans are not available. The base tier consists of six heart cakes, approximately 9", the middle tier is composed of pieces of cake put together to form a scalloped shape about 18" in diameter and the top tier is a 12" petal shape.

The tiers are covered with an egg white boiled icing, requiring no crumb coating. All decorating is done with the same icing, freehand lattice heart shapes, the "sotas" or lacework piped with a cone with a tiny cut tip, and simple star tube borders. The panels are attached to the separators with boiled icing (royal is too brittle). Then all tiers are placed in position.

When the ornament, cupids and bouquets are set on the tiers, switch on the lights! Here is Philippine decorating at its most dramatic!

Some decorating secrets

American decorators can learn much from the Philippine method. Boiled icing is easy to press out and allows you to complete the trim in a hurry. Lacework is much more quickly done than cornelli and gives a similar dainty look. Large star tube borders are very fast.

The painting that completes the flower trim gives a very unusual pretty effect. Another quick trim can be seen around the arched openings in the upper separator. A ½" strip of thinned food color is painted around the edge, then the panel is gently pressed in a mound of tinted granulated sugar for a sparkling border

For a breathtaking Philippine wedding cake, decorated more easily with modern decorating products, please turn the page.

The wonderful Philippine style

Golden Glow... *a Philippine-style masterpiece*

Yes, you can achieve this breath-taking, never-to-be-forgotten bridal cake! Just do it step by careful step and enjoy the architectural assembly. Then, at the wedding reception, light your radiant masterpiece for all to admire.

Make trims in advance

1. Make the gum paste pieces for separators and ornament first. Use Philippine gum paste, page 159, and *Celebrate! VI* patterns. You will need 1½ recipes. Roll out yellow-tinted gum paste to about ⅛" thickness and cut all the panels and ornament roof.

For round and oval "windows," roll out untinted gum paste thinly and form over halves of 3" plastic ball molds and 4½" egg molds. Trim off ½" up from base of molds and dry. Mold dome over a 4" ball mold, using full depth of mold. Cut a "U" shaped opening to accommodate electric plug. While all of these are drying, mold curves of gum paste for ornament trim with the Baroque Mantle mold, trimming off small outer curves and top fleur-de-lis. Attach the curves immediately, back to back, with a second group of curves, using royal icing as glue. You will need twelve finished curves. Secure two fleurs-de-lis back to back and dry on top of ball mold for finial on dome. Now mold three Baroque Angelicas and while still wet, secure with royal icing to lower oval openings on panels for base separator. Shape wings to follow curves of ovals.

For other three panels of bottom separator, shape thinly rolled gum paste over 2" bell molds and trim off to make six half-bells.

2. Make a recipe of Wilton gum paste, tint half of it yellow and cut out yellow and white flowers with the forget-me-not cutter. The fast way to do this is to roll out a small piece of gum paste, stamp out many flowers, then place them on soft foam and press the center of each flower with the round end of a modeling stick. Attach the oval and round windows to the backs of the separator panels with royal icing. Attach bells to fronts of remaining lower separator panels.

Edge openings with tube 1 beading. Attach gum paste flowers and ribbon bows to all panels with royal icing. (Flowers do not need to be completely dry.) Pipe a tube 2 dot in center of each flower.

Trim seven Harvest Cherubs with flowers, attaching with royal icing.

3. Use the Philippine method and royal icing to make flowers to trim the tiers. Twist about two dozen 5" lengths of florists' wire together, separate the ends and pipe tube 5 pistils

Please turn the page

CONSTRUCTION OF BASE TIER AND SEPARATOR

63

with royal icing. When these are dry, separate the wire stems, soften the icing (add one tablespoon corn syrup to one cup of icing) and pipe the petals with tube 81. Vary the flowers by first piping tube 1 stamens on some of the pistils, by piping a double row of petals on some, and by using tube 55 for petals of smaller flowers. Traditionally, these daisies are piped upside down, with the pistil at the bottom as you hold the end of the wire above, but holding the pistil upright gives just as fast a result. Make a bend in the end of the wire and hang the flower, upside down, on a wire rack to dry. Repeat the process for many blossoms.

Form six large bouquets with ribbons for the base tier by twisting stems together and wrapping with floral tape. Make six smaller bouquets for the middle tier. Clip off stems of remaining flowers to use for top tier trim.

Add wiring and assemble panels

Plastic pillars and separator plates give strong support to the tier separators.

1. For bottom separator, use two 9" hexagon plates and six 7½" Corinthian pillars. Screw a 40 watt appliance bulb into a wired electrical socket. Securely tape the socket to the center of the upper separator plate. We used silver-colored cloth tuck tape, available at hardware stores. Assemble the pillars and plates, using a little royal icing to make sure the pillars will not shift. Wire the electrical cord to one pillar, letting the remainder of the cord extend from the base of the pillar.

Run a heavy line of *boiled* icing down the lengths of two adjacent pillars and gently press a panel into position. Use plenty of icing. Continue adding panels, alternating oval window and bell-trimmed panels. With *boiled icing* and tube 15, pipe triple lines of shells to cover seams, then pipe a row of shells around base of separator.

2. For upper separator use two 8" round plates, six 10¼" pillars and four Stud Plate sets. With a pliers, clip off two of the projections from each plate, leaving two directly opposite each other. Fill in the spaces with the four stud plates, gluing securely, and making sure the projections and stud plates are evenly spaced. Fit a wired electrical socket with a long slender 40-watt display case bulb and tape it to the center of the upper plate just as you did for the bottom separator. Assemble plates with pillars and wire remaining cord to one pillar. Attach panels with boiled icing and trim with shells.

3. For ornament, use a 6" round plate, six legs from the Crystal Clear set and twelve stud plates. Prepare plate by gluing six stud plates to the plain side, evenly spaced. Glue six stud plates to the under side of the gum paste roof section so they line up exactly with the separator plate. Attach a cherub with royal icing to center of plate.

Attach gum paste supports to top of roof with royal icing. Fit a wired electrical socket with a 40-watt appliance bulb. Carefully insert bulb into hole in roof and secure socket to gum paste supports with short lengths of popsicle sticks and tape. Wire cord to one leg and let remaining wire extend from base of leg.

Secure panels to ornament and cover seams with triple tube 15 shells using boiled icing. Pipe shells around

FINISHED
BASE
SEPARATOR

base of ornament and at top of panels. Run a line of royal icing around dome, and set on roof. Attach gum paste curves in upright position at edge of roof with royal icing. Secure fleur-de-lis on top of dome.

Prepare the tiers

With all detailed preparation out of the way, the decorating is a breeze!

1. Bake the tiers, each two layers for a finished height of about 4″. For the base tier, bake six 8″ two-layer round tiers. For center tier, bake a two-layer 15″ hexagon, and for top tier, bake a two-layer 12″ hexagon. Fill and ice all the tiers in buttercream, or use egg white boiled icing as the Filipinos do. Using a 9″ hexagon pan as a pattern, cut a support for the lower separator from 4″ thick styrofoam. Ice with royal icing.

2. Cover the two upper tiers and the six 8″ cakes with "sotas" or *Philippine lacework*. This is a very fast and effective trim. Fill a cone with a tiny cut tip with boiled icing. Cover the sides, then the tops by jiggling your hand as you press out tiny waves and curls. Thin icing if necessary with a few drops of water. When the tiers are covered, go back and add a little more lacework on the top edges.

3. Cut the cake boards, using pans as patterns. For two upper tiers cut double thicknesses of corrugated cardboard. Cover with gold foil. Make a pattern for the base board from six 8″ circles. Set circles in position around the iced styrofoam base. Trace them, then add 2″ all around to form a petal shape. Cut this pattern from triple-thick corrugated, taped together, grains running in opposite directions. ⅜″ plywood is even better. Cover with gold foil and edge with a ruffle. Glue satin ribbon to curved edge.

4. Assemble base tier on board, support in center. *Use boiled icing for all trim.* Pipe tube 32 shells around base of bottom tier. Above them, pipe double scallops or "cords" with tube 20. Attach lower separator to center support with royal icing. Set two upper tiers on their boards. Edge base of middle tier with tube 22 "C's." Edge upper tier with tube 16 zigzags. Insert dowel rods in all tiers for support (see page 20.). Attach the upper separator to the middle tier with icing. Attach ornament to the top tier. Allow wires to extend to back.

The tiers are now ready to transport to the reception table.

Finishing is fun!

1. Set base tier on reception table. Place large bouquets in position and attach two little plastic doves beside each bouquet.

2. Attach middle tier to top plate of lower separator with royal icing. Pipe a row of tube 15 boiled icing shells at top of lower separator.

3. Attach top tier to upper separator, then add tube 15 shells to top of separator. Trim ornament at top and base with gum paste flowers. Add unstemmed flowers to sides of top tier and attach doves to top of tier. Place bouquets and cupids on middle tier. Plug in the lights and watch the scene light up with a golden glow!

This lavish masterpiece serves 356 guests. The beautiful ornament will be treasured by the bride.

Decorator's secret: First of all, don't be afraid! Read all the directions through carefully before beginning, then follow them *in order* as they are printed. Allow time, far in advance of decorating to make the trims.

Practice the "sotas" or lacework in advance. You'll be surprised and pleased at how quickly this dainty trim can be done with boiled icing.

DDLE SEPARATOR

ORNAMENT CONSTRUCTION

FINISHED ORNAMENT

Arabesque

...a bridal dream cake lavished with lace and delicate lattice

Lattice and lacy wings trim the most ethereal wedding cake crowned by an airy little lattice temple. Only basic techniques and careful planning are needed to create Arabesque.

1. Pipe the dainty drop flowers in royal icing with tubes 191, 224 and 225. Use varied tints of blue.

Using *Celebrate! VI* patterns, pipe twelve lace wings and the pieces for the top ornament with egg white royal icing and tube 1. For dome on ornament, grease a 3″ ball half-mold with solid white shortening. Mark mold in six sections and fill each section with lattice, then pipe beading to define sections and finish edge. When thoroughly dry, place mold in a warm oven for a few minutes and gently push off dome. Tape all other patterns to a stiff surface, cover with wax paper, pipe the designs and dry flat.

2. Construct the ornament. Using patterns, cut lower and upper bases, side wall support and roof from rolled gum paste. Dry thoroughly. Secure all pieces with royal icing. Stack lower base, upper base and wall support, centering each carefully. Glue small plastic doves to hands of Card Holding Cupid and attach figure to center of wall support. Ring base with flowers. Pipe a line of icing against edge of wall support and set one wall section in position. Pipe icing against adjacent edge of wall support, and on one side of first wall section. Set second wall section in place. Continue until all wall sections are standing, then cover seams with beading. Dry, then pipe a line of icing on top of wall and set roof on it. Attach dome. Edge roof and upper base with tube 1 beading. Attach leaves to roof and lace wings at wall sides with dots of icing. Trim completed ornament with flowers.

3. Bake, fill and ice the four tiers. Base tier consists of two 16″ round layers plus a 16″ top bevel. Second tier is made up of two 12″ layers, each layer 2″ high. Third tier is an 8″ round layer topped by an 8″ top bevel. Top tier is a two-layer 6″ round. Assemble on sturdy cakeboard with 10″ separator plates and 7½″ Corinthian pillars.

Divide and mark the tiers—16″ tier into sixteenths, 12″ and 8″ tiers into twelfths, top tier into sixths.

4. On 16″ tier pipe bottom shell border with tube 21, two borders that define bevel with tube 16. Drop string guidelines to define garlands and top of lattice at lower side of tier. Pipe zigzag garlands with tube 15, then pipe and over-pipe again to build up, pausing between pipings to let icing set. Do lattice, beaded edge and dropped string above with tube 2. Cover lower edge of lattice with tube 13 zigzags and add tube 14 fleurs-de-lis. On bevel surface, pipe tube 17 zigzag garlands and rosettes, then trim with tube 2 string.

5. On 12″ tier, pipe tube 17 shell borders at base and top. Drop guidelines and pipe tube 17 zigzag garlands, tube 2 string trim and tube 16 rosettes. Mark a circle with a 2″ cookie cutter above every other garland and outline with tube 1 tiny scallops.

6. Trim 8″ and 6″ tiers with tube 16. Pipe shell borders and zigzag garlands (garlands on 6″ tier will be covered with flowers). Drop strings on 8″ tier and pipe bows on 6″ tier with tube 2.

Attach bridal couple to ornament plate and set within pillars. Now trim entire cake with flowers, covering garlands on 6″ tier. Add leaves piped with tube 65.

7. Complete trim at the reception site. Attach lace wings with dots of icing to 12″ and 8″ tiers. Crown the cake with the airborne ornament. Arabesque is a big cake—three lower tiers serve 216, top tier 16.

It's such a versatile trim—lattice can add rich texture to a handsome cake for Dad or make a dainty frame for flowers on Mom's cake.

A cake for Dad

1. Pipe roses and buds with tube 114 and dry. Roll out marzipan, cut the oval with *Celebrate! VI* pattern and glaze. Pipe the message with tube 2. Now bake and fill a 9″ x 13″ sheet cake and ice with chocolate butter-cream. Transfer patterns to top and sides of cake.

2. Draw up three upright shells at each corner of cake and add curved shells and rosettes at top. Pipe a tube 18 shell border at base. Place the marzipan oval on cake top. Build up a base for lower edge of lattice designs on sides by piping a line with tube 16, then over-piping it with tube 14, and again with tube 13. Do the same on sides of design, tapering to top edge. Pipe lattice with tube 2. Add a final piping on all four edges with tube 13.

Build up outer long edges of lattice design on top of cake, then pipe lattice and finishing lines just as for side lattice. Edge oval with tube 13 shells. Complete decoration by piping top shell borders and fleurs-de-lis with tube 17. Attach roses on mounds of icing and trim with tube 67 leaves. Dad will love it! Serve to 24.

Look how Lattice

Decorator's secret. Work in a cool room when you pipe chocolate buttercream lattice. This is a good design for a groom's cake too.

A cake for Mom

A lattice frame surrounds a rose bouquet to tell her how you love her!

1. Pipe roses and buds with tube 104 and dry. Bake and fill a two-layer 9″ x 13″ sheet cake. Use a firm pound cake recipe. Cover the cake with rolled fondant as described on page 52. Transfer frame pattern to cake top.

2. Do outer edge of frame with four lines of piping—first tube 6, then 5, then two final lines with tube 4. Pipe a tapering wedge shape from each outer corner to center oval. Let dry. Drop lines of icing for lattice with tube 2, spacing slightly farther apart at outer edge of curved frame, and setting closer at oval. Edge with tube 2 beading, then pipe tube 1 scallops around oval. Pipe tube 18 upright shells all around base of cake, then trim with tube 3 dots and scallops. Pipe a spray of tube 3 stems within frame, add a tube 101 bow, and arrange roses on mounds of icing. Finish with tube 66 leaves and present to Mother. She'll be delighted! Serve to 24.

can dress up a cake!

HOW THE EXPERTS DO IT: AMY ROHR

New flowers in gum paste

Use your Flower Garden cutters to create many splendid new flowers. Amy Rohr shows you on page 72 how to make the showy day lily and a new rose. Below are descriptions for the cakes that set them off.

Day lilies for Dad

1. Make the beautiful lilies as directed on page 72. Twist stems together to form three clusters of two or three flowers, each with leaves. Cut out plaque from rolled gum paste, using *Celebrate! VI* pattern, dry flat, then pipe message and bead edges with tube 2.

2. Bake, fill and ice a two-layer 10″ square cake. Divide sides in fourths and mark about 1″ down from top edge. *The star tube side border is most effective.* Pipe a tube 16 bottom shell border, then pipe tube 26 curves, scrolls and hearts using marks on upper sides as guides. Center the scrolls with tube 16 fleurs-de-lis. Drop tube 13 strings below scrolls and top with stars.

3. Attach plaque to cake top and

70

insert three Flower Spikes in cake. Arrange lily clusters in spikes and present to a delighted Dad. Serves 20.

Wild roses for Mom

1. Make wild roses as shown on page 72 and twist stems together to form sprays. Cut pieces for base and support from rolled gum paste and assemble as pattern shows. Make gum paste plate by using a small saucer as mold. When dry, paint freehand decoration with thinned food color and an artist's brush. Pipe "Mom" with tube 1.

2. Bake a two-layer 9″ x 13″ sheet cake and a single-layer oval cake. Ice and assemble. Starting about 1″ in from each corner, divide long sides of sheet cake into fifths, short sides into fourths. Mark about 1″ up from base. Pipe a tube 16 bottom shell border. Pipe ruffled curves from mark to mark with tube 104, then top with swags. Use tube 13 for fleurs-de-lis at points. Finish the cake with tube 104 fluted borders.

3. Attach spray of flowers to plate, and secure plate to support with royal icing. Set on cake. Insert a Flower Spike in top of oval cake and two spikes in sheet cake, and arrange sprays. Mother will be charmed with this sweet confection. The flowery plate will be a lasting souvenir. Serves 30.

Decorator's secret. Fluted borders are quick & pretty to pipe with a petal tube. Use a shell motion, holding flat side of tube against surface.

READ THROUGH the Flower Garden booklet for general instructions, then follow Amy Rohr's procedures for the fun of making these new blooms. Use Wilton gum paste, page 158.

How to make Day Lilies

1. Cut six petals from thinly rolled gum paste with the lily leaf cutter. Texture a petal by pressing it on the violet leaf mold. Lay petal on soft foam and ruffle the edges by rolling with a modeling stick. Assemble three ruffled petals in a 2½" plastic lily nail, brushing tip of each with egg white to attach. Add three more petals, then make a hole in the throat of the flower with pointed end of a stick. Prop the petals with cotton and stick the nail in styrofoam to dry.

2. For yellow stamens, cut a 5" length of heavy wire and surround with six 1¾" pieces of fine wire, taping to secure. Insert the fine wires into tube 2 for red tips. Brush the inner throat of the flower with shaved pastels, then insert stamens through center hole. Dip a tiny piece of wet gum paste into egg white and smooth to base of flower to secure wire stem.

3. Cut out a leaf with the tulip leaf cutter and slice into five strips. Dip an end of wire into egg white, lay on a strip, and curve leaf with your finger.

How to make Wild Roses

1. These are made in a similar method to the briar rose, but cut the flowers from gum paste *at least ⅛" thick*. Roll with a stick to enlarge, then lay on a number 5 nail and pinch centers of petals with pointed end of a stick and your fingers. Cut calyx, curl points, then assemble stem, calyx and ball. Flower need not be thoroughly dry before assembling. Brush center with white pastels, pipe a tube 3 dot in center and surround with smaller dots. Insert clipped artificial stamens with a tweezer.

2. Make bud exactly as for briar rose. Cut calyx, lay on thick foam and press with rounded end of stick to cup. Cut leaves with small rose leaf cutter, attach wire stems to backs with egg white, and assemble in threes.

Decorator's secret. Tint florists' wire by mixing food color and water in a long pan. Soak wires for a moment or two, dry on wax paper. Sun will fade.

Remember—join two *dried* pieces of gum paste with a tiny piece of wet gum paste dipped in egg white—or use royal icing. Join two wet gum paste pieces, or one wet and one dry, by brushing with egg white.

First Prize winners

IN THE CELEBRATE! VI CAKE CONTESTS

To each a check for $250.00 and a handsome ribboned medal

Our sincere thanks to all of you who submitted entries. Every cake showed charm
and imagination and we only wish that each could have won a prize.

For more prize-winning cakes,
please turn the page.

CAKES FOR CHILDREN: *Dolores McCann*

This lavish graduation cake was created for her daughter by Dolores McCann of Oxford, Ohio. "You've come a long way, baby" is its title. The graduate is shown on a tiered cake in various stages of her life—first as an infant in a cradle, as a pinafored little girl holding a doll, as a blue-jeaned teen-ager with roller skates, and finally, as a graduate in a beautifully draped gown. All the figures, the cradle, the carefully made stairway and flower bouquets are in gum paste. Congratulations to Dolores for an ambitious, imaginative cake.

CAKES FOR MEN: *Helen Siskosky*

"Cake decorating is a challenge to creativity" writes Helen from Berkley, Michigan. Certainly she has met that challenge in this cake that shows her husband in his portable ice shanty fishing on a frozen lake. The ice is a sheet of poured hard candy, the fish and structure of the shanty are gum paste, and the figure is gum paste too, molded in a People Mold and modified to resemble her husband. The stage for this winter scene is a 12″ x 18″ sheet cake. Congratulations to Helen for re-creating a scene in meticulous and charming detail.

2ND PRIZE: *Shirley Manbeck*

Any child would be delighted with this springtime scene! Mama duck is baked in an egg-shaped pan with beak modeled in marzipan. Her feathers are piped with leaf tubes. The ducklings are figure piped in royal icing and the cattails are gum paste. The cake is 18" square with a bank built up at the rear, and a piping gel pond. A check for $100.00, a ribboned medal and congratulations to Shirley Manbeck of Austin, Texas, our second prize winner.

TWO DAINTY DOLL CAKES EACH WIN A THIRD PRIZE

3RD PRIZE: *Bradley Jones*

This elegant doll starts with a fruit cake baked in a wonder mold and covered with marzipan and rolled fondant. Head and torso of the doll are molded in gum paste. The elaborately draped skirt, stole and fitted bodice are made of rolled gum paste. Even the curled coiffure is gum paste! A medal, a $50.00 check and best wishes to Bradley A. Jones of Indianapolis, Indiana.

3RD PRIZE: *Judith Thompson*

The skirt of this sweet doll is baked in the wonder mold, then covered thickly in buttercream and formed into folds. A pattern piped with tube 1 dots covers the entire dress. A triangle of tulle is draped around shoulders, then trimmed with dots and fringe. Congratulations, a ribboned medal and a $50.00 check to Judith Thompson of Indianapolis, Indiana.

2ND PRIZE: *Lana Shumney*

This 1980 Corvette is most realistically formed! The body of the car is a 12″ x 18″ sheet cake, resting on a block of styrofoam. Curves were added with cake baked in a book pan. The top is an 8″ square cake with sides beveled, the wheels are big cookies. Lana iced the cake smoothly, then used round tubes to pipe details and tube 16 for stars on top and wheels. Congratulations to Lana Shumney of Wickliffe, Ohio. We're sending her a $100.00 check and a second place medal.

3RD PRIZE: *Kevin Work*

A bottle of fine champagne and an elegant glass to drink it from! Kevin Work shaped this prize winner from fruit cake and covered it with plastic icing (the Australian equivalent to rolled fondant). The label and grape leaves were cut from gum paste and the grapes made in the pulled sugar method. All the decorating is done in the meticulous Australian manner. We're pleased to send a third place medal and a check for $50.00 to Kevin Work of Redwood Park, Australia.

HONORABLE MENTION: *Shirley Neeley*

A mother owl and her baby perch on a cake decorated for a taxidermist. Shirley hand-modeled the owls in royal icing. "At first they didn't look like much, but when I started adding the feathers with tube 101, they seemed to come alive!" The log is baked in a soup can, the short projections are marshmallows. Violets, grass and realistic piped mushrooms complete the scene. Congratulations and a check for $10.00 to Shirley Neeley of Springfield, Ohio.

Readers share their decorating adventures

HERE ARE JUST A FEW views of outstanding decorating by our talented readers. To each we're sending our congratulations, together with a token of appreciation.

1. *Norma Woolridge* of Lovington, Illinois, created these 10″ x 12″ rooms and all their Victorian furniture from gum paste! The fireplace and foyer floor and staircase are veined to look like marble, the dining room floor is made to look like wood parquet. Norma crafted all the "mahogany" furniture to scale—the roses in the foyer are just over ⅛″ in diameter!

2. *Kay Jean May* of Clawson, Michigan shares an idea for a cake for a Cub Scout banquet. The four hexagon tiers display Color Flow badges of rank and achievement. Surrounding 10″ cakes are topped with caps baked in the ball pan.

3. *Mrs. A. L. King* of Mile End, Australia sends us an entire Christmas dinner on a 10″ octagon cake! The china, glassware, vegetable-garnished turkey, pudding and cake—even the vase with a tiny rose—are carefully molded from gum paste. The table is covered with a rolled fondant cloth edged with dainty royal icing lace.

4. *Tina Joramo* of Great Falls, Montana built a very authentic chuck wagon entirely from gum paste and Color Flow. Even the axles and wagon tongue are gum paste. Tina set her wagon on an oval plaque, so it can easily be lifted off the 9″ x 13″ cake.

5. *Linda Reid* of Houston, Texas made eight little gum paste figures with the five-year-old mold, dressed them to represent various nationalities and set them on a 12″ cake. Centering the cake is the "world," baked in a ball pan.

6. *Deb Schroeder* of Davenport, Iowa shows us how to make a cute, quick "ham." Bake a cake in the egg pan, trim off wide end, then ice. "Cloves" are piped with tube 3, "fat" and "bone" with tube 44. A good cake for Easter or just for fun!

STEP INTO OUR NEW

SugarPlum Shop

IT'S FILLED WITH BRILLIANT CAKES FOR HAPPY BIRTHDAYS

Star on wheels, directions, page 79

Make it very
personal...
express the interests,
occupations or hobbies
of the birthday child
whether he's 7 or 70
on a

beautiful birthday cake

What a perfect opportunity to make someone happy! Make a birthday cake that could belong only to the birthday child! Express his favorite sport or occupation or the things he likes the most. Here are dozens of cakes in the Sugar Plum Shop to inspire you to decorate your own very special cake for a very special person on his birthday.

WE START with a half-dozen cakes that feature the birthday child himself, full color and in action! These life-like little gum paste figurines look like porcelain, and last nearly as long. Not only will they trim a once-in-a-lifetime birthday cake—they'll serve as beautiful souvenirs of the birthday party.

Little leaguer, at left

1. First mold the figure in the ten-year-old child mold following directions in the People Mold booklet. Dress the figure in clothing like he usually wears. After figure is dressed and made up, cut a 1" circle of thinly rolled gum paste for cap. Mold it over the head and groove with a stick for seams. Pipe hair with tube 13, then cut visor of cap freehand and attach. Paint stripes with thinned food color.

2. Model a ½" ball of gum paste, groove with a stick and attach to hand while wet with egg white. Model a 1⅛" circle of gum paste, about ⅛" thick, into glove. Groove for fingers.

Mold gum paste over a marshmallow for rock the figure leans on, then model a few smaller rocks. For bat, form a ¼" cylinder, 3" long and taper. Paint tapered end with food color.

3. Ice a 6" separator plate with royal icing, leaving edges uncovered. Rough up with a sponge, secure large rock and figure, then smaller rocks and tube 233 grass.

4. The cake is a 10" square two-layer stage for the figure. Bake, fill and ice, then pipe tube 3 message on front. Pipe tube 32 shells at base and edge with tube 13 zigzags. Drop tube 13 string curves from top edges of two sides and back, then pipe a tube 19 rope border and corner fleurs-de-lis. Set little leaguer in center of cake and light with candles. Smudge a little food color "dirt" on figure! Serves 20.

Star on wheels, page 77

1. Mold the gum paste figure in the 10-year-old child mold. Her flirty skirt is a 2½" circle, center cut out with large end of a tube. Slit the back and wrap around hips, meeting at back and arranging folds. Turtle neck starts with a 2" x 3" rectangle of rolled gum paste. (See page 13, instruction booklet.) For skate boots, wrap a ⅝" strip of gum paste around foot, meeting and trimming at front. Lace with tube 1s. Roll gum paste ³⁄₁₆" thick, cut out wheels and bumpers with tube 11 and attach. Add tube 13 hair-do.

2. Cut out a 5" circle of rolled gum paste, secure to a 6" separator plate and edge with tube 3 beading. Attach figure to plate.

3. Bake, fill and ice a two-layer 10" round cake. Pipe message with tube 2 (see page 38). Do base border with tube 78 curved shells, and ruffly garlands with the same tube. Trim garlands with tube 52 stars and add a tube 53 reverse shell top border. Set figure on cake and insert candles. Present to a delighted little girl and serve to 14.

Please turn to page 84 for more suggestions on gum paste figures.

Make your piped message a part of the cake design

Many highly skilled decorators feel unsure of themselves when it comes to piping script or block printing on a cake. Here are a few tips from the *Celebrate!* staff to help you.

NO SUBSTITUTE FOR PRACTICE. Take just a few minutes a day for concentrated work—you'll be surprised at your improvement. Tape wax paper over alphabet patterns and trace with icing and a small round tube. Then print or write messages freehand on the back of a pan. Keep a steady even light pressure.

CONSISTENCY OF ICING is important for effortless strokes. Thin boiled or buttercream icing with white syrup or gel so it flows easily out of the tube. Hold the tube just above the surface and let the lines drop, never dig in. Keep cone as horizontal as possible.

PLAN AHEAD! The message should be piped first. Letter it on a cake circle or paper. Pipe over your message for practice, then pipe it on the cake.

PRESS WITH YOUR FINGERS, not the whole hand. Keep the movement going. Use a small cone for ease.

SCRIPT IS EASIER for many decorators than block printing. You will develop your own style of script with practice. Vary it by practicing script initials, using patterns.

IN BLOCK PRINTING, pipe vertical strokes first, then curves. Go back and add diagonals and horizontals.

USE THE WINDOW METHOD. Pencil your message on paper, repeating until you get the design and spacing you like. Carefully cut out the letter areas, leaving windows for the words. When icing on the cake crusts, lightly lay the windowed paper on the cake and print or write your message within windows. Keep the cut-out words within your vision as you pipe. Add ascenders, descenders and flourishes after you pick up the paper.

FOR MESSAGES ON SIDE of cake, be sure to keep the cake at eye level.

He's your hero!

Surprise your policeman on his birthday with a three-dimensional portrait of a moment in his busy day. Here's a birthday cake he'll never forget!

1. Mold the gum paste figure in the man People Mold. After torso, head and legs are posed and dried, dress him in the clothing he wears for work. Page 16 in the People Mold booklet gives you basic directions and patterns—add appropriate emblems and trims. The night stick is a 2½" long cylinder. For hat, attach a ¼" strip around head, then glue on a 1" circle for top. Finish with a ⅛" strip, a freehand visor and tube 1s royal icing trim. Add tube 13 hair.

The little girl is molded in the 4-year-old child mold. Cut a 2" circle for her skirt, cut out center with large end of a standard tube and slit up the back. Attach to figure, modeling pleats with your fingers. Page 14 in the People mold booklet gives general directions. When figure is complete, add tube 13 hair and a bouquet of tiny drop flowers.

2. Attach a 4½" circle of rolled gum paste to a 5½" separator plate. Edge with tube 2 beading and attach figures. Using *Celebrate! VI* patterns, cut emblem for side of cake and assemble. Trim with tube 1s.

3. *Quick borders with star tubes* trim the cake. Bake, fill and ice a 10" two-layer square cake. Secure emblem to side with icing and print message. Trim corners and base of cake with tube 22 curved shells, then fill in base with tube 17 rosettes. Pipe top shell border with same tube. Set your little tableau on cake top and edge the plate with tube 14. Add the candles and serve to 20 admiring guests.

Put your Mr. Fix-it on a pedestal

This cake will show him just how much he means to you! It's planned for the man who works with his hands —whether he's a carpenter, plumber, mechanic or a just-wonderful handy man.

1. Mold the figure in the man People Mold and dress him in appropriate clothing. Page 16 of the People Mold booklet shows you how. Put a suitable tool in his hand. (Wrench pattern is in *Celebrate! VI* Pattern Book.)

The tiny birthday cake is gum paste about ¾" high and 1½" in diameter. Ice and trim it with tiny tubes just like a real cake. Cut a 2" circle from rolled gum paste for cake plate and secure it to a 3" Grecian pillar. Use pattern to cut the scroll, curl wide end and attach while wet to the pillar. Letter with tube 1s.

2. Secure a 4½" circle to a 5½" separator plate and attach figure and pillar. Edge with tube 2 beading.

3. Bake, fill, ice and assemble a two-layer 10" round cake and a single-layer 6" cake. Print message on 10" cake (see page 38). *Star tube borders* look lavish, but are very easy to do. Divide 10" cake in twelfths, mark at base, and pull up tube 18 triple columns, adding curved shells at top of two outer columns, a star at center one. Fill in base border with tube 18 stars and pipe a tube 17 top shell border. Center tube 190 drop flowers between columns and pipe tube 66 leaves.

On 6" cake, pipe a tube 16 base shell border, then add curves, scrolls and upright shells with the same tube. Finish with stars, then pipe a tube 15 top shell border.

Put figure on cake top, insert birthday candles and bring in to your cheering audience. Serves 17.

For more views and news of gum paste figures, turn to page 84.

PLACE A FIGURINE, just like her, on her birthday cake. She'll treasure it for many birthdays to come. Use the woman People Mold for these entrancing gum paste figures.

Is she a gardener?

1. Mold the figure and dress it in her usual working attire, patches and all. Page 16 of the People Mold instruction booklet gives basic directions. *Use Celebrate! VI* patterns for the shirt and pants, trimming as necessary. Pipe her tousled hair-do with tube 13. For the carrot, make a hook in one end of a 2½" length of florists' wire. Hand-model the carrot over the other end of the wire. Length is 2¾." Groove with a knife. Put the hook over the wrist of the finished figure, then conceal it with tube 1 curly foliage. Add smudges of food color "dirt."

For the hat, cut a 2¼" circle from thinly rolled gum paste, shape the crown, then add a string of gum paste for ribbon. Hand model the little trowel—handle is ¾" long, shield-shaped blade is ¾" long, ½" wide.

2. Cover a 5½" plate with a 4½" circle of green gum paste. Attach figure to plate, then pipe tube 3 beading and tube 233 grass.

3. Bake, fill and ice a 12" round, two-layer cake. Pipe an appropriate message on the side with tube 2. Pipe reverse shell borders with tube 20 for bottom, tube 17 at top. Center the cake with the figure. Edge plate with tube 16 shells. Serves 22 guests.

For your favorite nurse

1. Mold the figure as People Mold booklet instructs and dress it, using *Celebrate! VI* patterns. Wrap a ½" strip of gum paste around foot for shoe, meeting and trimming at back. After figure is dried and made up, pipe simple hair-do with tube 13, set on a ⅜" x 2" strip of gum paste for cap, then pipe side-brushed bangs. Cut a circle with large end of tube 2A for the tray, lay on soft foam and press with large end of a standard tube to

indent. The little cups on the tray are cut with tube 12, indented with tube 7. Attach cups to tray, tray to hand.

2. Secure a 5½" circle of rolled gum paste to a 6" separator plate, edge with tube 3 beading, then attach figure. Pipe tube 104 roses and buds in royal icing. Dry, then mount on wire stems. Pipe tube 67 leaves on wire. (See page 113.)

3. Bake, fill and ice a two-layer 9" x 13" cake. Pipe message with tube 2. Divide short sides of cake into fourths, long sides into sixths, and mark midway on sides. Pipe a tube 19 shell border at base, then pipe tube 79 swags from mark to mark on sides. Add tube 3 strings above and below swags, then pipe tube 17 upright shells and rosettes. Finish with a tube 17 top shell border.

Set figure, on its plate, on cake top. Arrange roses around plate, then form a bouquet with remaining roses and place on cake board. This will be a second souvenir for the birthday child. Serve the cake to 24.

Please turn the page for more tips on making the gum paste figures.

Make a unique ornament for your tennis star's cake

It's easy to use your own artistry to put together an ornament that complements a special interest. For this one, we glued two plastic rackets to the back of a "Queen of the Courts" figure. Glue a ribbon bow to each handle, add drop flower trim.

1. For the cake, pipe tubes 34 and 224 drop flowers. Bake, fill and ice a two-layer, 8" square cake. Pipe tube 2 message in a curve on cake top. Divide each side into thirds and mark midway on sides.

2. Pipe a tube 17 base shell border. Drop string curves for garlands and lattice from mark to mark, then pipe tube 16 zigzag garlands. Let set up, then over-pipe the garlands. Fill in with tube 1 lattice and finish with tube 1 beading. Do top shell border with tube 16.

Set ornament on cake top and trim with a few more drop flowers. Add flowers to lattice curves and pipe tube 65 leaves. Insert a curve of candles behind ornament. Serve the cake to twelve guests.

Quick & Pretty

Your own touches make it very personal

If you haven't experienced the fun of creating perfect little gum paste figures with People Molds, make your first one to put on a birthday cake. Anyone who receives a cake like this will be overwhelmed with delight. The three-part molds make it easy to mold a figure in proportion—and the figures are in lifelike proportion, one to another, too, if you'd like to mold a group. Before you start, read the booklet that comes with the molds.

Some gum paste tips

As the *Celebrate!* staff has worked on gum paste figures over the months, we found shortcuts to share.

Use the updated method in the Wilton gum paste recipe on page 158 in this book. It makes the gum paste much easier to mix. Add just enough sugar to make the paste the consistency of bread dough, and a little sticky. Store at least overnight, then break off a piece, knead in additional sugar until pliable and no longer sticky.

To smooth out seams in dried figure, paint with egg white and smooth in a little gum paste to fill. This is much easier than using royal icing.

To attach arms, dip a tiny piece of wet gum paste the same color as clothing in egg white. Press to shoulder area, then attach arm and smooth seam.

Set the figure on a separator plate to make it easy to lift off cake and save. Here's how we do it. For all standing figures insert lengths of stiff florists' wire into legs. Let the wire extend about an inch from foot of one leg. Stick wire into styrofoam block and prop figure to dry. Cover the plate with a circle of gum paste. Decide where you want the figure to stand and make a hole in the plate with a heated ice pick. Insert wire in hole, bend flat on underside of plate and tape. We also use tiny pieces of wet gum paste brushed with egg white under feet.

Make it just like him —or her

Position the figure in a characteristic pose. See the relaxed slouch of the baseball player and the proud stance of the skater! Apply make up and hair-do to resemble the person. Dress the figurine in the clothing usually worn for work, sport or hobby. Accessories such as the oversized wrench and carrot provide humor.

After you've created one figurine, we know you'll go on to many more adventures. For scores more ideas, read the gum paste chapters in Volume Two, *The Wilton Way of Cake Decorating.*

Yes, it's your golfer...

blasting his way out of the rough! To make it look like him, we painted the clothing on a plastic figure with two coats of thinned royal icing.

1. Bake, fill and ice a two-layer oval cake. Cover top with green icing and pat with a sponge. Mark a curve on cake top and mound up a little icing at rear of cake. Pipe message on side with tube 2.

2. Pipe tube 8 ball borders at bottom and top. Drop double tube 5 strings on side and add dots with same tube. Set golfer on cake top and pull up long grass with tube 233. Dandelions are just yellow tube 13 stars. Add candles and present to a delighted golfer on his birthday. Serves twelve.

Is he a Wild West fan?

If you want to make him a really smashing birthday cake, decorate this one. The bucking horse and cowboy in Color Flow is an adaptation of Remington's "A Sun Fisher."

1. Start in the same manner as you would for any Color Flow design. Tape pattern to a stiff surface and tape wax paper smoothly over it. With tube 2, outline only the main areas of the design as *Celebrate! VI* pattern indicates. Pattern is like a "paint by numbers" design. Let outline crust. Have all tints of thinned icing ready and in cones with tiny cut tips. Work quickly, from left to right, to flow in the colors, allowing them to blend naturally as you move from one tint to the next. When design is completely dry, turn over and reinforce with tube 13 zigzags. Dry again, turn right side up and over-pipe main outlines, reins and bridal with tube 1. Pipe mane and tail with tube 13.

2. Bake, fill and ice a 10″ square two-layer cake. Pipe grass on cake top with tube 1, message with tube 2. Starting 1″ in from each corner, divide cake into fourths and mark midway on side. Make a second series of marks at base of cake, midway between first. Connect marks to form triangles. Fill in triangles with tube 17 stars. Above them, outline with tube 103, then tube 4. Accent with tube 13 shells. Pipe a tube 15 rope border at top. Set "Sun Fisher" on cake top on mounds of icing. Serves 20.

Does he love elegance?

This beautiful beveled cake is for him.

1. Cut the circular frame for the letters from ¼″ thick rolled marzipan, using *Celebrate! VI* pattern. For message and small hearts tape patterns, word by word, to sides of 6″ round pans. Tape wax paper smoothly over them and pipe tube 2 outlines. Carefully fill in the letters with thinned icing, letting each set up a little before going on to the next. After small hearts are dry, turn over and outline and fill in again.

Tape large heart pattern to a 10″ curve. Outline, then fill in very thinly. When dry, pipe tube 1 name and beaded edge.

2. Pipe tube 103 wild roses with tube 1 centers and air-dry within curved surface. Bake, fill and ice a two-layer 10″ round cake and set on an iced 14″ bevel. Divide bevel in twelfths.

3. Pipe shell-motion border at base of bevel with *curved ribbon tube* 79. Use the same tube to pipe scallops from mark to mark. Accent with tube 3

string. On side of 10″ cake, pipe three tube 3 scallops within each scallop on bevel. Add dots, then pipe a tube 6 bulb border where bevel and 10″ cake meet. Pipe tube 79 scallops on cake top, then add tube 353 border.

Set marzipan ring on cake top and attach the Color Flow words with icing. Attach small hearts on inner edge of ring, then insert tapers. Attach large heart to cake side. Form cascades of flowers and trim with tube 66 leaves. Serves 26.

Just what he always wanted!

A birthday pie!

And what a pie! It's baked in a 9″ x 14″ casserole, and bears his portrait painted on the crust! Follow the *Celebrate! VI* pattern for the portrait of the farmer, or modify it for a different occupation.

Here's the method of this new-old painting technique. Make his favorite two-crust pie. While rolling out the crust, cut flowers with the forget-me-not cutter, pitchfork and hand that holds pitchfork. We filled ours with six cans of apple pie filling. (It has a smoother texture than fresh fruit.) Cut out the pattern like a stencil, lay it on the unbaked pie and mark with a pin. Cut slits around outer edges.

Prepare the "paint." *For rather large areas* like the pants, stir together one egg and two teaspoons of water. Divide into small portions and tint with liquid food color. *For outlining* and small details like checks on shirt, mix one egg yolk and one teaspoon of water, then divide and tint.

Pre-heat the oven and do painting quickly. Using a small artist's brush, first paint all outlining in brown, then do checked shirt and all small areas. Paint pitchfork and flowers. Last of all, do green hill, then pants. Attach flowers, pitchfork and hand with egg mixture and put pie in oven to bake.

Surround your fresh-baked portrait with birthday candles. Cut the pie into twelve big rectangular pieces.

Quick & Pretty…in two delicious flavors

He can have his cake, and eat it, too, if you bake two cakes in his favorite flavors.

1. Bake two single-layer cakes in 10″ round pans. We used chocolate and lemon flavors. Make a recipe of Snow-white buttercream. Tint one half yellow and flavor with lemon. Stir in four tablespoons of cocoa into the other half. Ice the cakes. Cover each with poured fondant. Let set for several hours.

2. Cut each cake into eight pieces,

and reassemble on trays, alternating flavors. Using stabilized whipped cream (page 158), pipe tube 22 fleurs-de-lis and tube 18 shells to cover seams. Add a birthday candle. Each cake provides eight heroic pieces, or 16 more modestly sized.

Quick & Pretty… and fit for a king

A chocolate cream pie is many a man's idea of paradise. Here's how to dress one up for his birthday celebration. Using your favorite recipes, prepare the crust and filling. With tube 1C, pipe spiral "crowns" of stabilized whipped cream and top each with a candied cherry. Set a birthday candle in the center of the pie.

Make him happy

Is his garden his pride?

Trim his cake with sunny zinnias, or choose the flower he likes the best.

1. Pipe zinnias in advance. Pipe a tube 5 dot in the center of a number 7 nail. Pipe petals with tube 101, starting at outer edge. Add a tube 13 star in center, top with tube 1 dots.

2. Bake, fill and ice a two-layer 9″ x 13″ cake. Transfer *Celebrate! VI* oval pattern to cake. Pipe message with tube 1. Run a tube 6 line of icing around top edge, side corners and base of cake. In contrasting color, pipe tube 15 shells at base of cake on cake board. Within the line, on sides of cake, pipe a second shell border. On cake top pipe shell border and curve within piped line. Finally pipe center rows of shells on top of piped line. Attach cluster of flowers and trim with tube 66 leaves. Add a curve of candles. Serve to 24.

A badge of love

Tell him that he's tops with an oversized ribboned medal made of sparkling hard candy.

1. Mold five small hearts in candy molds. For large heart, oil the inside of a 4½″ high heart cookie cutter. Lay on oiled foil and pour in the hot syrup. Let harden, then remove cutter and peel off foil.

For the ribbon, pipe two contrasting strips about 5″ long on wax paper with tube 789, ribbed side up. Pipe a third strip with tube 1D. Pipe a strip about 5½″ long with the smooth side of tube 789 up. Use buttercream icing. Freeze the strips.

2. Bake, fill and ice a 9″ x 13″ two-layer cake. Pipe simple shell borders using tube 20 for base, tube 47 for top. On wax paper set the three ribbed strips together, sides touching. Trim to 4¾″, then round lower corners. Trim smooth strip to 5″. Assemble on cake top with large heart. Add tube 2 beading, message and "eyelets." Attach small hearts and insert a row of birthday candles. Serve to 24 guests.

A rainbow of wishes ...Quick & Pretty

1. Bake, fill and ice a two-layer 9″ x 13″ cake. With a ruler, mark a horizontal line on cake top, 2½″ up from one long edge. Pipe message with tube 3. Pipe tube 225 drop flowers.

2. With a spatula, ice the upper part of the cake top with blue icing. Let set up. Mark *Celebrate! VI* pattern for top curve of rainbow. Mark circles with a 3″ cookie cutter. Pipe the rainbow with tube 2B, starting with the top band of color and continuing down side of cake. Fill circles with tube 16 spirals, adding rays to sun. Pipe sun features with tube 13 and name on side with tube 3.

3. Pipe a tube 17 top shell border. Following marked line, pipe tube 233 "grass" on cake top and around base of cake. Add flowers and candles. Serve to 24.

91

THREE SWEET WAYS to honor a lady of any age on her birthday.

A "floating" greeting

Perform this slight of hand with a gum paste frame, a bit of tulle and dainty drop flowers!

1. Pipe royal icing drop flowers with tubes 17, 20 and 96 in the star method. (Don't turn your hand while squeezing.) From rolled gum paste, cut a 5½" circle for base and two oval frames using *Celebrate! VI* pattern. Cut an oval of tulle and brush egg white on one still-wet gum paste frame. Lay tulle on frame, brush again with egg white and cover with second frame. When dry, letter your message with royal icing and tube 1.

2. Assemble the ornament by attaching frame and two little cherub figures to base with tiny pieces of wet gum paste dipped in egg white. Cover frame on both sides with flowers on dots of royal icing. Add more flowers around cherubs, tube 65 leaves, and tube 2 beading around base.

3. Bake, fill and ice a two-layer 10" round cake. Use boiled icing to cover the cake with fast Philippine lace work (page 65). Do the bold curved base border with tube 32. Trim with flowers and tube 66 leaves. Set ornament on cake, insert a curve of candles in Push-in holders and your enchanting little cake is finished. It's even prettier when the candles are lit and seen flickering through the tulle. Serves 14.

Quick & Pretty painted flowers

Everyone will say you're an artist when they see this pretty masterpiece!

1. Bake and fill a two-layer 12" hexagon cake. Cover with egg white boiled icing, using two coats for a smooth surface (boiled icing is best for this technique).

2. Stroke icing on cardboard to use as a practice board. Mix liquid food color with water for paint. You will need pink, yellow and green, each in deep and pastel tints. With *Celebrate! VI* pattern in front of you, paint flowers freehand with an artist's brush, first doing the petals in pastel tints, then adding tiny lines and dots in deep tints. Do leaves in the same way. Adjust colors by adding water or more food color.

3. Transfer pattern to cake, marking only the centers of the flowers. Paint the cake. Pipe message with tube 2 and do simple borders with tube 13 scallops, shells and stars. Add birthday tapers and serve your masterpiece to 20 guests.

Decorator's secret. For a finer-flavored icing, substitute ¼ cup of liquid drained from canned fruit cocktail for ¼ cup of water in egg white boiled icing recipe.

Quick & Pretty daisy ring

1. A simply pretty little cake is ringed with fluffy daisies. Any lady will love it. Pipe the daisies in boiled icing with tube 102. Add tube 5 centers and dry within smallest curved form.

2. Bake, fill and ice a two-layer 8" square cake. Mark a deep curve on top and side for placement of daisies. Pipe message with tube 2, then do base border with deeply curved tube 17 shells. Attach daisies with dots of icing, insert the candles and you're ready for the party! Serve to twelve.

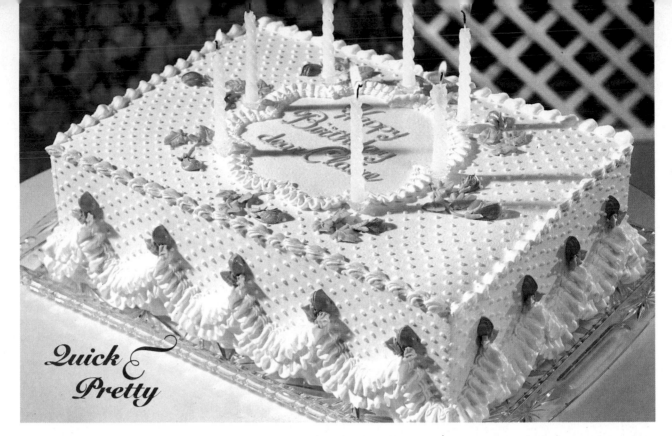

Quick & Pretty

Is she sentimental?

Decorate this sweet hearts-and-flowers cake for her birthday.

1. Pipe drop flowers in advance with tubes 193, 129 and 225. Make the butterflies in the Color Flow method. Tape patterns to a stiff surface, tape wax paper smoothly over them and outline with tube 1. Fill in areas with thinned icing. When dry, pipe a tube 6 line on wax paper for body, insert wings and artificial stamens and prop to dry.

2. Bake, fill and ice a two-layer 10″ square cake. Gently press the 7½″ pan from the Heart Mini-Tier set on top for pattern. Fill in green icing with a spatula, pipe tube 2 message.

3. Run a tube 12 line around base of cake. Cover with clusters of tube 67 leaves, then attach flowers. Pipe a tube 17 top shell border. Cover heart area with leaves and flowers. Let butterflies alight on mounds of icing and surround heart with candles. Serve to 20.

Decorator's secret. Be sure to use thinned icing for piping leaves, and pull them up to perky points.

Is she a weight watcher?

Indulge her on her birthday with candy, whipped cream and chocolate—but keep the servings small!

1. Mold the cute little cupcakes in summer coating in candy molds (see page 146). Unmold and top with tube 18 swirls and tube 5 cherries.

2. Cover a two-layer 9″ petal cake with chocolate buttercream. Use tube 21 to pipe the ruffly garlands and swirls in stabilized whipped cream. Letter your message with thinned food color on a card and tie it to the birthday taper. Cut into 16 slender pieces.

Does she like to sew?

She'll love the dainty "dressmaker" details on this easy-to-serve sheet cake. The rosebuds are piped right on the cake.

1. Bake, fill and ice a two-layer 9″ x 13″ cake. Press a 6″ petal pan on top to define scallop pattern. Pipe message with tube 2. Starting 1″ in from each corner, divide long sides of cake into fourths, short sides into thirds.

2. Pipe bottom shell border with *specialty tube 63,* then use *star-cut tube 88* for the quick double ruffles. Pipe tube 63 shells at top edge. Use the same tube to pipe the ruffles on cake top. Pipe short tube 2 stems from scallops, then pipe the rosebuds with just one shell motion of tube 63. Pipe more rosebuds on sides of cake and trim with tube 66 leaves. Dot the cake with tube 2 for dotted swiss effect. Serve to 24.

Decorator's secret. Looking for an idea for a get-well cake, welcome-neighbor cake, or just a you're-so-special cake? Modify any of the three pictured here.

Sugar Plum
BIRTHDAY CAKES

For Grandma and Grandpa...their favorite things

Pearls, perfume and roses

delight Grandma's feminine heart.

1. Pipe the roses and buds with tube 104. Cut and freeze a little piece of cake 1½" x 2", 1" thick. Cover top and three sides with buttercream, chill, then brush with piping gel. Let set up, then outline tiny heart with tube 1 and boiled icing. Fill in with thinned icing. When dry, ice fourth side and paint with gel. Ice a flat sugar cube for stopper of bottle. Pipe a tube 4 circle on bottle top and set stopper on it.

2. The 9" two-layer heart cake is iced in buttercream with all trim in boiled icing. Mark *Celebrate! VI* patterns for pearls and heart on cake top. Divide each side of cake into sixths and drop string guidelines.

3. Pipe tube 1s cornelli. Do base shell border and garlands with tube 17, strings and graduated pearls with tube 2. Outline heart on cake top with tube 1 and flow in with thinned icing. Do graduated pearls and stems for roses with tube 4. Edge heart with tube 2 beading, write message with tube 1. Now arrange perfume and roses on cake, add tube 66 leaves and candles. Serves twelve.

96

Grandpa collects stamps

He'd love an album cake with two choice first-day-of-issue covers.

1. Do the covers in Color Flow, outlining *Celebrate! VI* patterns with tube 1. Fill in with thinned icing, first white, then colors. Pipe details with tube 1, lettering and beading with tube 1s.

2. Bake and ice a 10" square, single-layer cake. Groove three sides with a comb for pages, then pipe message with tube 2. Run tube 5 lines around book, attach covers. Serve to ten.

Golf, gardening, a pet pipe

…add up to an ideal day for Grandpa.

1. Hand model the pipe, golf balls and tees from marzipan. Pipe is 4" long, stem and bowl done separately. Balls are 1" in diameter, tees 1¼" long. Cut a 5" circle of rolled marzipan. Glaze all marzipan. Pipe zinnias as shown on page 91.

2. Bake, fill and ice a 10" round, two-layer cake. Pipe message with tube 2. *Star tube borders* are simple and attractive. At base of cake, pipe a tube 22 star every 1". Frame with tube 16 "C's". Do top shell border with same tube. Set marzipan circle on cake top and edge with tube 16 scallops. Arrange Grandpa's favorite things on circle. Serves 14.

Happy birthday! Call in the clowns!

Clowns are just the embodiment of all the silly, delicious fun that goes on at a birthday party, so make the cake a clown for a hilarious celebration.

A great big clown...

is baked in a bowling pin pan!

1. Fill the two halves of the cake, insert toothpicks to hold securely together and trim 1½" off the base. Set upright on wax paper. Ice with buttercream. Mark lines for collar and waist. Figure pipe arms and build out legs, front and back, with tube 2A. Smooth with a spatula.

2. Pipe big feet with tube 2A and top with tube 9 balls. Do ruffles around ankles with tube 127, then cover cake with tube 15 stars up to waistline. Pipe tube 127 ruffle, then cover arms and body with tube 15 stars and add another ruffle for collar. Figure pipe hands with tube 9. Use tube 9 for mouth and nose, tube 3 for eyes, eyebrows and ears.

3. Pipe derby with tube 2A crown, tube 9 brim. Do hair with tube 233. Add the finishing touches—stemmed drop flowers and a contrasting tube 1 edge around ruffles. We set our clown on a single-layer 12" cake edged with tube 16 shells. The message is piped with tube 2. Serve to 20.

Decorator's secret. See how a contrasting edge with a small round tube perks up a petal tube ruffle.

Clown faces...

grin and grimace from the sides of a hexagon cake.

1. Bake, fill and ice a 9" two-layer hexagon cake. Bake and ice six half-eggs in the egg cupcake pan. Cover with poured fondant. Pipe message on cake top with tube 2, then edge with tube 16 shells.

2. Pipe a mound of icing on cake side, then secure a cupcake by pushing a piece of plastic drinking straw through cupcake into cake, placing it where nose will be piped. Give each clown face a tube 78 ruffled collar. Use your imagination for their expressions. Pipe features with round tubes, hair with tube 233 and hats with tube 9 or 4B. A few drop flowers add a festive touch. Pipe tube 2C candle holders on cake top and push

in candles. Serve to twelve.

A clown for each guest

...makes the party very merry!

1. Bake a small wonder mold cake for each guest and cover with poured fondant. Dip marshmallows in fondant and toothpick to cake for legs and head.

2. Figure pipe arms with tube 2A. Do white zigzags with tube 15, features and buttons with tube 3. Arrange the clowns on a serving tray, then pipe tube 2B hats and insert candles. Give the clowns stemmed drop flowers to hold, or paper banners glued to toothpicks. Light the candles and bring in the clowns!

98

Eight little dolls circle her birthday cake

They're just as pretty as she is. Here's another way to use the pans you already own to make a spectacular cake.

1. Bake, fill and ice with buttercream an 8″ round, two-layer cake and nine cakes baked in blossom pans. Cover blossom cakes and 18 marshmallows (nine large and nine small) with poured fondant. Pipe drop flowers with tubes 224 and 225. Divide round cake into eighths and mark 1″ above base.

2. For the dolls, thread a fondant-covered marshmallow to a miniature marshmallow to a large marshmallow (for bodice) on a toothpick. Insert in a blossom cake. Edge bases of cakes with tube 13 shells, then pipe tube 102 scallops. Cover bodice with tube 13 stars, pipe arms with tube 2A. Do puffed sleeves with tube 13 stars. Collars are piped with tube 103, features with tube 2, hair with tube 13. Add circlets of flowers on heads, and form bouquets.

3. On round cake, do bottom and top borders with tube 16 shells. Drop tube 103 scallops from mark to mark and add tube 16 stars at points. Form eight flower cascades at top edge. Center one doll on cake top and surround with eight dolls. Trim all flowers with tube 349 leaves and insert candles. The little dolls are favors for the guests to take home. Slice the round cake into ten pieces.

Smiling faces and funny hats!

Use your Fancifill and egg cupcake pans for this little spectacular! Each face is a portrait of a party guest.

1. Bake and ice a cake in the Fancifill pan. Bake, fill and ice six egg cupcakes. Cover cupcakes with poured fondant, then cut about ½″ off bases for stability.

2. Cover sides of Fancifill cake with tube 17 stars, then pipe a tube 32 shell border at base, a tube 20 zigzag border at top. Set cupcakes on mounds of icing on top. Pipe tube 4 features on cupcakes, set on ice cream cone hats, then do tube 13 hair. Trim hats with small round and star tubes and drop flowers. Insert tapers, light them and serve the Fancifill cake to twelve. The faces may be given as party prizes.

Let's play dress-up!

Set a cute little plastic figure on a cake, add candles, tinted icing and colorful flowers to make a prize-winning birthday cake.

1. Pipe drop flowers with tubes 224 and 225. Bake, fill and ice an 8″ square, two-layer cake. Cover sides thickly with tinted buttercream and groove with a decorating comb. Letter message with tube 2. Do base border with tube 32 curved "C's." Add a tube 17 top shell border. Place figure and candles, then add flowers and tube 65 leaves. Twelve little girls will love it!

Decorator's secret. A separator plate will often serve as an ideal cake tray. For the doll cake, we used the plate from an Arched Pillar set.

If you are using marshmallows in the construction of a cake, set them out, uncovered, overnight. They will be firmer and easier to handle.

Quick & Pretty

Happy Birthday
Billy !

Add a toy to a quick, colorful cake and you'll add an extra present and a lot of fun!

Ride 'em cowboy!

1. Bake, fill and ice a two-layer 9" x 13" cake and ice a single-layer 6" square cake. Set 6" cake on a 7" square separator plate and assemble with sheet cake. Pipe message with tube 2. Starting 1" in from each corner, divide long sides of sheet cake into fifths, short sides into thirds. Mark about 1" down from top edge.

2. Pipe loops on sides of sheet cake from mark to mark with tube 362. Do rope border at base with tube 199, top shell border with tube 18. On 6" cake, do bottom shell border with tube 18. Set Cowpoke figure on cake and fill in cake top with tube 17 stars. Run a tube 362 line around top edge, forming loops at corners. Line up the birthday candles and the party's on! Sheet cake serves 24. Save the little square cake for the birthday child.

Rocking horses and building blocks…

add excitement to a quick-to-do tier cake.

1. Bake, fill and ice the two-layer round tiers, 12" and 8". Assemble with ABC separator set. On 12" tier, pipe a tube 18 bottom shell border. Pipe tube 16 strings and rosettes and a top shell border with the same tube. Edge separator plate with shells.

2. On 8" tier, cover sides with tube 2B. Pipe tube 18 rosettes at base of cake, tube 16 shells at top. Insert tall tapers, place plastic balloons within pillars and rocking horses on top. This big cake serves 32 party guests.

Teddy's my favorite!

1. Pipe tube 193 buttercream drop flowers and freeze. Bake, fill and ice a two-layer 10" cake. Pipe message with tube 3 (see method on page 38). Divide side in sixths.

2. Pipe tube 16 stems on side of cake and tube 67 leaves. Attach flowers. Pipe a tube 32 bottom shell border, a tube 16 shell border at top. Set Honey Bear on cake top and frame him with a curve of birthday candles. Serve to 14 guests.

Cut it up to make it cuter, below

Turn a sheet cake into three colorful pennants for a young sportsman's birthday party!

1. Tape *Celebrate! VI* pattern to a stiff surface, tape wax paper over it and

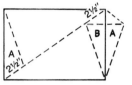

Cut cake in half diagonally. Use trimmings for small pennant.

outline the letters with tube 2 and Color Flow icing. Fill in with thinned icing and dry.

2. Bake a single-layer 9" x 13" cake and cut as diagram shows. Set each pennant on a cake board, same size and shape. Ice, then rough up with a damp sponge. Pipe a tube 16 shell border at base of each. Set pennants on serving tray, attach letters on dots of icing and add candles in Push-in holders. The plastic football player completes the colorful scene.

Two larger pennants serve ten, the small pennant belongs to the birthday child.

Pizza girl

1. Model the cute cartoon-like figure in marzipan first. Tint a recipe of marzipan (page 157) in the colors you'll need and have fun. Cut a 5" circle for base and a 2¾" circle for pizza from rolled marzipan. Attach base to a 5½" separator plate with egg white. Scatter bits of tinted marzipan on pizza and use red food color thinned with a little gin or vodka for sauce.

Model onions, peppers, sausage, tomatoes, cheese and olives. Roll marzipan in a cylinder about ¾" in diameter. Cut off ¾" slices to model everything except the olives (cut ⅜" slices). Roll pieces between your palms into balls, then form with your fingers. An orange stick is a good tool for adding details.

Model horseshoe-shaped legs first and let dry about half an hour before assembling figure as diagram shows. For apron, attach a 1" x 2" strip of rolled marzipan to waist and paint stripes with thinned food color. Assemble completed figure on base and surround with vegetables. Glaze, then pipe tube 3 royal icing beading on plate. Pipe tube 13 hair, tube 3 eyes and tube 1 mouth.

2. Bake, fill and ice a 10" round two-layer cake. Divide cake into sixths and mark midway on side. Drop string guidelines for scallops, then pipe message with tube 2. Fill area from base to scallops with tube 16 stars. Pipe a tube 19 top star border. Center the figure on the cake top, frame with candles and arrange vegetables, sausage and cheese at base of cake. Serve to 14 teenagers. The figure is a souvenir for the birthday girl.

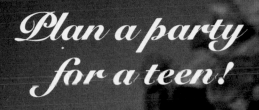

*Plan a party
for a teen!*

Burger boy

1. Model the figure just like the Pizza girl. Halves of hamburger bun are modeled from 2¾″ circles, ¼″ thick. Put together with lettuce, meat and cheese cut from rolled marzipan. Cover a 5½″ plate with a 5″ circle of marzipan and assemble figure on it, allowing legs to dry for about half an hour before attaching other pieces. Glaze, then pipe tube 4 beading on plate. Pipe hair and features just like Pizza girl.

2. Bake, fill and ice a two-layer 9″ x 13″ cake. Mark position of figure, then pipe tube 2 message. Cover sides of cake with tube 1D. Do base shell border with tube 18, top border with tube 16. Set figure on cake top and insert a curve of candles. Serve to 24.

Decorator's secret. When painting marzipan, always thin food color with a white liquor such as gin or vodka. This will dry quickly and prevent color from bleeding.

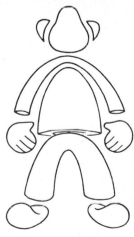

Pear-shaped head about 1″ high. Model ½″ ears.

Arms are cylinders flattened in center.

Bell-shaped body about 1½″ high.

Horseshoe-shaped jeans, 1½″ high.

Feet are 1¼″ ovals flattened at back.

A beaming bunny, page 106

1. Cut ears from stiff paper using *Celebrate! VI* pattern and ice. Put bunny together with icing, using toothpicks as necessary. Diagram shows how. Set on a 7″ separator plate. Fill in all crevices with icing and figure pipe round cheeks with tube 10. Cover with tube 16 stars. Pipe eyes and nose with tube 10, mouth with tube 3. Whiskers are icing-covered pieces of spaghetti.

2. Pipe drop flowers with tubes 2D, 2E, 1B and 225. Bake, fill and ice a two-layer 9″ x 13″ cake. Write tube 2 message and pipe tube 18 shell borders at bottom and top. Mark curves on sides and attach flowers. Set bunny on cake. Pipe tube 233 grass on plate and form a bouquet for him to hold. Pipe tube 3 stems and trim all flowers with tube 66 leaves. Insert a ring of candles. Sheet cake serves 24 —cut bunny into eight servings.

A cheerful turtle, page 107

This spritely pet is constructed with a cupcake and a half-ball cake!

1. Set ball cake on a 6″ cake circle and ice. Use iced styrofoam for legs, or a firm pound cake with dowel rods inserted to support ball cake. Construct as diagram shows on a 6″ separator plate. Attach a flattened marshmallow for tail. Mark turtle shell with 1″ and 1⅜″ heart cutters. Pipe tube 2A neck, eyes and cheeks. Run a tube 12 line around edge of shell. Now outline the hearts with tube 2 and cover the turtle with tube 15 stars. When finished, over-pipe mouth and pipe eyelashes and tongue with tube 3. Glaze eyes with corn syrup.

2. Bake, fill and ice a 10″ two-layer cake. Pipe message with tube 13. Do tube 1D borders, edge with tube 13 shells. Set turtle on cake top and pipe tube 13 scallops around plate. Serve 10″ cake to 14, turtle to seven.

A chocolate running shoe

is easily carved from an 8″ x 4″ x 4″ loaf cake. See the diagram below.

1. Chill the cake before carving the shoe. Set on a cardboard cake base the same size and shape and cover with buttercream. Build up the tongue and heel areas with extra icing. Pipe base of shoe, top edge and stripes with tube 45. Add tube 2 beading. Do grommets with tube 6, laces with tube 44.

2. Pipe tubes 131, 224 and 225 drop flowers. Bake, fill and ice a 10″ square, two-layer cake. Write message with tube 2. Divide sides in fourths and pipe a tube 16 shell border at base. Top with fast ruffled garlands piped with *drop flower tube 106*. Pipe a tube 17 reverse shell top border. Set shoe on cake top, line up candles and present to your runner. 10″ cake serves 20, cut the shoe into six slices.

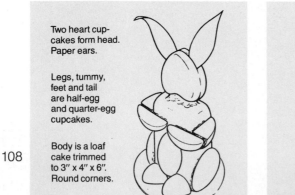

Two heart cupcakes form head. Paper ears.

Legs, tummy, feet and tail are half-egg and quarter-egg cupcakes.

Body is a loaf cake trimmed to 3″ x 4″ x 6″. Round corners.

Shell is half-ball cake, cupcake head.

Legs are cut from a 4″ square, 2″ high. Taper to 1½″ at back, then groove.

Carve shoe from a 4″ x 4″ x 8″ cake.

Top view

Side view

Celebrate!®

JULY AND AUGUST

Get set for the fourth!
Directions, page 118

Hurray for the 4th

109

Stars and Stripes

Quick & Pretty

CUBE CAKES are always intriguing and talked about. Decorate one or both of these little charmers for a Fourth of July picnic or barbecue. Start each cake by baking three 6″ square layers, each about 1¾″ high, so when filled, the cakes will be 6″ high. Ice smoothly in white buttercream.

Stars and stripes

1. Sugar-mold 32 stars in candy molds. (Add edible glitter to the mixture for sparkle.) Attach tube 190 drop flowers to wire stems (page 113). Mark two opposite sides of cake into seven stripes, each ⅞″ wide.

2. Pipe the stripes with tube 16 stars, alternating red and white. Cover the two other sides with blue stars, then press in the sugar stars. Insert a Flower Spike in center of cake, par-tially fill with icing and insert a taper and the flowers. Slice into 12 pieces.

Just stars

Just as showy as Stars and Stripes, and very fast to decorate. Just transfer *Celebrate! VI* pattern to cake sides and fill in the areas with red and blue stars. Add red, white and blue candles and serve to twelve.

Decorator's secret. Tint buttercream in strong colors like these ahead of

for the 4th

time. Colors will deepen as they age for a few hours. Finished icing should be lighter than the final effect you want. The texture of the piping makes the colors look more vivid. Add a little cinnamon or an extra drop of flavoring to red icing to mask the sometimes bitter flavor of the food coloring.

Flag waving clowns...

are fun to figure pipe! Do these right on the cake, or on a block of styrofoam covered with wax paper.

1. Pipe the clowns. Since these are rather large figures, use a mixture of half royal, half figure piping icing. For clown with large flag, insert a toothpick into cake or styrofoam and pull up an upright tube 6B shell on either side of it for body. Pipe legs with same tube. Pipe a tube 102 neck ruffle, then a ball for head with tube 1A. Use tube 6B to pipe an upright shell for hat. Insert flag, then pipe tube 4B arms, tube 102 ruffles at wrists and ankles, tube 7 hands and tube 12 feet. Pipe clown on edge of cake the same way. Finish both clowns with tube 2 hair, features and balls and tube 13 eyes.

2. The simple cake is a breeze to decorate. Bake, fill and ice a 10″ round, two-layer cake. Cover sides with tube 2B stripes, then add rosette borders with tube 19. Serve to 14.

SHASTA DAISY "ALASKA"

BACHELOR BUTTON

PETUNIAS
IN VARIETY

"BOUQUET" ZINNIAS

Apple Blossom

Star Joy

Cherry Tart

Summer garden flowers...

Old favorites piped with a new twist

IT'S AMAZING how tinted icing, a flower nail and decorating tubes can produce a flower that looks just like one growing in a garden. Of course, the secret is your own skilled hands.

Here's a mini-course on piping four of summer's loveliest flowers. We've discovered some new ways to make the flowers mimic nature's own—and some beautiful new varieties to pipe. *All are shown in actual size.*

Shasta daisy "Alaska"

Nothing says summer like a daisy! Pipe these flowers in a number 8 flower nail. The saucer shape will give the petals pretty curves. Cover the nail smoothly with a square of foil, then *lightly grease the foil* with solid white shortening. This makes it much easier to release the dried flower.

For the fragile petals of the daisy, use boiled or royal icing, although in dry weather, buttercream is a possible choice. Starting at the outer edge of the nail, pipe a circle of tube 103 petals. Touch wide end of tube to nail and squeeze lightly, decreasing pressure as you move in to center. Pipe a tube 6 ball in center, then dip your finger in tinted sugar to flatten. Indent center with the round end of a modeling stick. Lift foil off nail to dry.

Bachelor button

These fluffy flowers are pretty on any summer cake and especially appropriate for a groom's cake. Attach a square of wax paper to a number 2 nail with a dot of icing. The nail will define the size of the flower. Pipe a tube 8 ball in center of nail. With deep-colored icing and tube 13, pull out a cluster of upstanding petals on the ball, holding tube straight up. Change to tube 15 and lighter-tinted icing to circle the ball with more rows of petals, slanting tube outward as you approach edge of nail. Slide paper off nail and place over a small curved form to dry. Use boiled, royal or buttercream icing. We used boiled icing for ease in piping.

Petunias in variety

Here's the all-time American favorite in three striking varieties. Boiled or royal icing is best for all, but buttercream may be used. Start by lining a two-piece 1⅝" plastic lily nail with foil. Lightly grease the foil.

APPLE BLOSSOM is a classically shaped petunia in an especially pretty pink. Pipe five tube 102 petals. Beginning in center well of nail and keeping narrow end of tube out, move up to edge, then back to center, jiggling hand to ruffle. Pipe a tube 14 star in center, tube 1 stamens.

STAR JOY begins with five petals piped just like Apple Blossom. With slightly thinned icing and tube 66, pull out a slender leaf with pointed end in the center of each petal. This forms the striking "star." Finish with a tube 14 star and tube 1 stamens.

CHERRY TART is a ruffled beauty with color-streaked petals. Fit a decorating cone with tube 103, spatula-stripe the inside with white icing, then fill with deep rose icing. Jiggle your hand for deeply ruffled petals, starting at outer edge of nail, going to center, then back to edge. Continue for a full, fluffy effect.

"Bouquet" Zinnias

A showy new mum-like variety. These are big flowers, a full 2½" across. Use boiled or royal icing. Line a number 8 nail with foil and lightly grease. Pipe a tube 10 ball in center, then cover entire surface of nail with icing. Starting on outside of nail, pull out circles of tube 101s petals, lifting cone as you work toward center. As you approach center, change to tube 349 for the last circle of petals. Finish with a cluster of tube 1 stamens.

Put flowers on stems...

to make pretty bouquets. *Only royal icing flowers* may be mounted on wire stems. Pipe a mound of green royal icing on a square of wax paper. Suit the size of the mound to the weight of the flower—tube 6 is right for a tube 103 rose. Insert a length of florists' wire straight up in mound, then brush icing up on wire to form a calyx. Turn wire upright and stick in styrofoam to dry. Remove wax paper and attach flower to calyx with a dot of icing. For stemmed leaves, pipe a dab of icing on wax paper. Lay a length of fine florists' wire on the dab, then pipe the leaf right over it, so center vein is directly over the wire. Dry.

Turn the pages to view a little gallery of summery flower-trimmed cakes.

Daisy

Pretty enough for a bride

…at an intimate wedding reception—easy enough to decorate just to surprise the family. The fresh-looking daisies make this summery cake especially appealing.

1. Pipe the daisy petals in two sizes with tubes 103 and 104 just as described on page 113. Use a number 8 nail and boiled or royal icing. Add tube 6 centers.

2. Bake and ice three tiers in the Mini-Tier pans. Set middle tier on a 6" cardboard cake circle wrapped in clear plastic. Assemble on serving tray using 5½" plate and one set of clear legs.

3. Trim this cake in just minutes! Pipe a tube 48 base border on all three tiers. Do top shell border on bottom tier with tube 16, on other two tiers with tube 14. Arrange daisies on mounds of icing. Serve to twelve.

Zinnia

A glowing centerpiece

Elegant enough for any important celebration. The beautiful Bouquet Zinnias are arranged to follow the curves of the petal-shaped cake.

1. Pipe the zinnias just as directed on page 113. Start with a tube 10 ball, then pipe outer petals with tube 101s, inner petals with tube 349. Finish with tube 1 stamens. Use a number 8 nail and boiled icing.

2. Bake and fill a two-layer 12″ petal cake. Ice smoothly in buttercream and set on serving tray. Lightly press a 6″ round pan in center of cake top to define pattern.

3. Pipe a tube 16 stem in center of each curve on side of cake. Pipe a tube 16 bottom shell border, then pipe deeply curved tube 21 shells. Outline curves on top edge with tube 18 swirls and pipe a rosette in center. Using marked circle as guide, pipe tube 16 swirls. Attach flowers on mounds of icing, then pipe tube 68 leaves. Serves 26 guests.

Petunia

One little cake…

makes a charming gift to delight a new neighbor, a friend just home from the hospital or for someone who's been especially considerate at work. Three make a showy centerpiece. Their petite 6″ size makes them especially appealing.

1. Pipe the petunias in boiled icing in the variety of your choice, or in three varieties—Apple Blossom, Cherry Tart and Star Joy. Directions are on page 113. Freeze or air-dry.

2. Bake and fill a 6″ round, two-layer cake. Ice with buttercream, then use boiled icing for decorating. Divide side into eighths and mark about 1½″ up from base. Drop string guidelines for ruffles.

3. Pipe a tube 15 shell border at base, a tube 87 shell-motion border at top. Use *star-cut tube 87* again to pipe the ruffles from mark to mark. This tube automatically adds a neat "rickrack" edging to the ruffle. Top ruffle with tube 15 fleurs-de-lis. Arrange petunias on mounds of icing, setting one or two in center on marshmallows for height. Pipe ruffled tube 67 petunia leaves. Each little cake serves six.

Bachelor button

With a man in mind...
decorate this handsome flowered
cake. The deep hues of the flowers
are set off by the white cake top and
framed by rich chocolate icing.

1. Pipe the bachelor buttons as
described on page 113.

2. Bake and fill a two-layer 9″ oval
cake. Ice top in Snow-white buttercream, side in Chocolate buttercream. (Add four tablespoons
of cocoa to a half-recipe of
Snow-white buttercream.)

3. In center of long sides of cake, pipe
a tube 18 fleur-de-lis. Use the same
tube to edge base of cake with stars.
At narrow ends of cake, pipe graduated curved shells. Do top border
with deeply curved tube 17 shells.
Pipe a cluster of tube 4 stems on cake
top. Spatula-stripe a cone fitted with
tube 65 with deep green icing and
fill with paler green. Pull out long
slender tube 65 leaves. Arrange
the flowers on mounds of icing
and serve to twelve.

Decorator's secret. This makes a
distinctive groom's cake. For more
servings, place the cake on a
chocolate-iced sheet cake.

BAKE A JUST-FOR-FUN cake, trim it with fast pretty flowers and present it to a friend or neighbor—or just surprise the family.

Bravo Bobby!

This bright cake boasts a circlet of flowers piped right on the cake!

1. Bake, fill and ice a 10″ round, two-layer cake. Mark top with an 8″ pan or cake circle and pipe tube 2 message.

2. Pipe tube 20 rosettes at base of cake and a tube 18 shell border at top. Pipe a circle of tube 20 stars on top. Pull out a five-petal flower on every other star with *curved ribbon tube 79*. Center the flowers with tube 4 dots. Serve to 14.

Welcome to our block

1. Roll out a third-recipe of marzipan and cut out flowers with daisy cutter. Cut yellow centers with tube 2A. Attach to flowers and dry within curved form. Cut out a circle of marzipan, using a 6″ pan for a pattern. Glaze all marzipan.

2. Bake, fill and ice a 9″ x 13″ two-layer sheet cake. Cover with Philippine lacework in boiled icing. (See page 65.) Attach circle to cake top with icing and write tube 2 message. Edge circle with tube 3 beading and arrange daisies. At base of cake, run a heavy line with tube 12. Add a daisy at each corner. Serve to 24.

Thank you!

An easy-to-decorate, easy-to-serve sheet cake looks very pretty with a flower garland framing the message.

1. Pipe drop flowers in buttercream and freeze or air-dry. Use tubes 2D, 194, 191 and 107. Bake, fill and ice a two-layer 9″ x 13″ cake. Mark top by lightly pressing with a 9″ oval pan. Write message with tube 2.

2. Use a shell motion with leaf tube 352 for bottom and top borders. Arrange the flowers in an oval garland, attaching with dots of icing. Trim with tube 349 leaves. Serve to 24 guests.

A different drummer
shown on page 109

This perky little fellow has a winning personality! He's all cake and 10″ high.

1. Bake all the cakes first. You'll need a two-layer 9″ x 13″ sheet cake as a stage, drum is a single-layer 6″ round cake. Drummer is constructed from four half-egg cupcakes—two for feet, two for head—two small wonder molds and a dozen miniature marshmallows.

2. Bake, fill and ice the cake. Divide long sides of cake into thirds and mark at base. Divide short sides into halves. Make marks on top edge midway between marks at base and connect to form triangles. Pipe all the blue lines with tube 45, then fill in the spaces with tube 15 stars. Finish with a tube 13 shell border at top.

3. Ice top and side of the 6″ cake and divide into sixths. Mark for triangles.

Pipe blue stripes with tube 45 and fill in with tube 15 stars. Chill the cake, then lay iced side down on wax paper and ice the bottom. Chill again.

4. Build the drummer on a 7″ separator plate. Set plate on cake top, supporting with a few dowels in sheet cake, clipped off level with surface. Ice all the cakes thinly. Set feet on plate, then wonder molds, iced together. Fill two half-eggs and toothpick together for head. Set on top of body and push a plastic drinking straw through head and body to plate. Pipe crossed shoulder straps and belt with tube 46. Fill in face with tube 14 stars, all other areas, including plate, with tube 15 stars. Pipe features with tube 3. Thread five marshmallows on a toothpick for arm and attach to shoulder with a toothpick. Cover arms with tube 15 stars. Pipe epaulets and hat trim with tube 14. Cut a freehand visor from light cardboard and push

into hat. Cover with icing.

5. Set drum on sheet cake in front of drummer and push a plastic drinking straw through it and into cake. Make drumsticks by spearing marshmallows with toothpicks. Cover with thinned icing and stick into hands. Pipe message with tube 4, then edge drum with tube 13 shells. Strike up the band and start the barbecue! Serve sheet cake to 24.

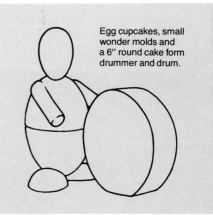

Egg cupcakes, small wonder molds and a 6″ round cake form drummer and drum.

Lacy and lovely for a 13th anniversary

Lace is the traditional gift for the 13th wedding anniversary.

1. Make trims in advance. Pipe drop flowers with tubes 224, 225 and 131. Mount some on wire stems (page 113) to form a bouquet. Cut two paper hearts, using *Celebrate! VI* pattern. Pipe the couple's names with tube 1 and glue hearts to hands of cherub figure. Trim with flowers and beading. Prepare a cake board for upper tier by tracing a 9″ hexagon pan on strong cardboard. Cover with foil and glue on six stud plates.

Tape patterns for lace wings and pieces to stiff cardboard and tape wax paper over them. Pipe about 100 lace pieces with tube 1s. Pipe wings with tube 1. When dry, turn over and over-pipe main lines with tube 1s.

2. Bake, fill and ice the two-layer tiers —a 12″ round and a 9″ hexagon. Place 12″ tier on serving tray and lightly mark position of twist legs by pressing with prepared hexagon board. Transfer scalloped pattern to cake top. Assemble tiers with six twist legs. Divide side of lower tier into twelfths and mark 1″ down from top edge. Make a second series of marks for garlands about 1½″ up from base. Drop string guidelines. On upper tier mark "13" pattern.

3. At base of lower tier, pipe a tube 16 shell border, then zigzag garlands. Trim with double tube 2 string and tube 13 rosettes. Pipe tube 1 cornelli lace. Add tube 2 beading.

4. On upper tier, outline "13" with tube 2 and dot with tube 1s. Pipe a tube 13 shell border at base, tube 4 bulb borders at corners and top edge. Drop string guidelines for zigzag garlands. Pipe with tube 16 and add double tube 2 string, tube 13 rosettes.

Glue Winged Angels to pillars and place bouquet. Set cherub on top, trim with flowers and trim base tier with flowers. Pipe tube 65 leaves. Attach lace last with dots of icing. Serve your exquisite cake to 34.

120

New in gum paste ...Water Lilies

For a July anniversary

Decorate this delicate cake with July's flower, the water lily, here newly formed in gum paste. For basic instructions, read the Flower Garden cutters booklet. Use Wilton rolled gum paste.

1. For large lily, clip the legs off the bowl of the Angel Fountain and cover inside of bowl with gum paste. Dry. Cut petals with Daffodil cutter, separate into three, roll to curl and secure around outside of bowl. Cut ten leaves with the Large Violet cutter, roll to elongate, and attach for second row of petals. For third row of petals, cut eight leaves with the Lily Leaf cut-

ter. Roll to enlarge, curl on a soft sponge, then cut a ½″ slit at base of leaf. Cross these two points to cup petal and secure to base of flower.

For small lilies, cut three shapes with the Small Daisy cutter. Roll each to enlarge, curl on a soft sponge, then assemble. Method is similar to method on page 18 of booklet. Pipe tube 1 royal icing stamens. Cut plaque, using pattern, and dry on a 10″ curved form. Pipe names and beading with tube 1.

2. Cut a 7″ circle from corrugated cardboard and cover with foil for plate for upper tier. Cover a 4½″ circle with

foil for base. Glue four 5″ Corinthian pillars, set close together, on base and plate. Bake an 11″ ring cake and a single-layer 6″ cake and cover with poured fondant. Assemble tiers on serving tray, using prepared pillars. Divide top tier into sixths, mark about ½″ down from top. Divide lower tier into tenths, mark 1″ up from base.

3. Pipe tube 16 base shell borders on both tiers. On base tier, pipe tube 103 curved ruffles below marks, then tube 16 garlands and fleurs-de-lis and tube 3 strings and hearts. Use same tubes for upper tier border. Attach lilies and plaque. Serves 18.

Send her off in style

As your indispensable secretary leaves for vacation, present her with a nosegay and a plea to hurry back!

1. With royal icing, pipe tube 104 roses and tubes 102 and 5 daisies. Mount on wire stems. Pipe tube 66 leaves on wire. When dry, twist stems together, frame with a doily and bow.

Pipe royal icing pencil on wax paper with a tube 12 line, a tube 7 point. Dry. Pipe rings for secretary's note pad on wax paper with tube 2.

2. Bake, fill and ice a 9" x 13" two-layer cake. Cut 5" x 7½" note pad from a 1" high cake. Set on cardboard cake base, cut to fit, and ice. Groove sides with a comb. Starting 1" in from corners, divide long sides of cake into fifths, short sides into thirds. Mark about 1½" up from base.

3. Set note pad on sheet cake, attach dried rings, then pipe tube 2 message. On sheet cake pipe a tube 18 bottom shell border, then ruffled garlands from mark to mark with *tube 78*. Pipe tube 16 rosettes and shell border at top, then tube 43 quick double scallops. Set nosegay on note pad and lean pencil against it. Sheet cake will serve an office crowd of 24.

For their fourth...books!

Give books for the fourth anniversary.

1. Bake two 11" x 15" single-layer cakes, and two small wonder molds.

2. To make the books, freeze one sheet cake, then cut into three 5" x 8" layers and stack. Assemble on 5" x 8" cake base. On one end, measure in 2" and mark on top. Cut a 1" slice up to the mark and stack as shown. Push four dowels into cake down to cake base and clip off level with top. Ice the top and back of the cake thickly with white buttercream and groove with a decorating comb. Ice sides of books smoothly, then cover front with four tube 789 stripes. Pipe tube 3 lettering and lines around binding of all books.

For the bookends, cut about one-third vertically off each wonder mold. Ice smoothly, then pipe tube 2 features and tube 14 hair-dos.

3. Ice the sheet cake. Pipe fleurs-de-lis and upright shells on sides, a star border at base, a shell border at top —all with tube 22. Set books and bookends on cake. Cut sheet cake into 16 slices, books will serve ten.

Lollipops for their sixth

For the sixth anniversary, candy.

1. Bake, fill and thickly ice a single-layer 12" square cake. Mark top with a decorating comb. Bake two cakes in 5½" Mini-Tier pans. Round the edges and ice with buttercream. When icing is set, boil white corn syrup for two minutes and pour over cakes.

2. On square cake, pipe dots of icing on gumdrops and press to cake for border. Pipe a tube 17 shell border at top. Position "lollipops," write tube 2 message, ring with halved gum drops and insert dowels. Add a ribbon bow and a bouquet of tooth-picked gum drops. Square cake serves 18, lollipops serve 6.

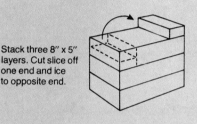

Stack three 8" x 5" layers. Cut slice off one end and ice to opposite end.

Happy-time cakes

Amber lace

Here's a new-old technique using Caramel sugar to spin a delicate tracery of glistening lace-like threads. With it, you can craft a cake tray, weave a little basket, even spangle a cake!

CARAMEL SUGAR
    1⅓ cups granulated sugar
    ½ cup white corn syrup
    ⅔ cup water

Blend all ingredients. Cook without stirring until syrup is amber and tests 320° to 330°F. Remove from heat. When bubbles disappear, syrup is ready to form the shapes.

Cover back of a tray, mold or pan smoothly with foil. Grease lightly with solid white shortening. Grease a teaspoon, dip into syrup to cover the back of it and move your hand quickly back and forth over the prepared form to cover it. Cool about five minutes, remove from form while still warm and allow to cool completely.

This recipe makes enough syrup to form two 12″ oval trays, or four baskets formed on blossom pans. Entire process takes about 20 minutes and may be done several days ahead. Line tray or basket with plastic wrap so cakes or candy will not stick.

The petits fours

Bake your favorite sponge or butter cake in a shallow sheet cake pan, cut in 1¾″ squares and cover with poured fondant. Pipe tube 2 stems, tube 63 rosebuds, tube 65 leaves.

The golden cake

Bake, fill and ice with buttercream a 10″ two-layer cake. Mark a 4″ circle on top and cover with a 4″ circle of foil. Cover the cake with Caramel sugar. Remove foil, pipe a tube 22 shell border at base and frame with tube 14 zigzags. Pipe tube 14 shells around top circle and set basket (formed over blossom pan) on cake. We filled it with marzipan fruits (page 104). Serve to 14.

Celebrate!

Apple cakes
to take to school.
Directions, page 135

Your party was so much fun

HAVE A HAPPY TIME! Invite your friends to an autumn get-together. A colorful, imaginative cake will set the theme for the party fun.

A sweet scarecrow...

says summer is over and it's time to plan for fall's excitement. Would you believe that he's baked in the bowling pin pan and dressed in buttercream?

1. Bake a cake in the bowling pin pan, using a firm pound cake recipe. Put together with icing, toothpick to secure and cut ½" off base. Set on an 8" plate, make grooves for legs and ice thinly with buttercream. Mark waistline. Skewer two marshmallows and insert for arms.

2. Ice from top to marked waist with chocolate buttercream. Ice pants with spatula. Pipe jacket edges with tube 8. Fill in with spatula. Fill in arms. Pipe collar, sleeves and scarf with tube 2B. Pipe buttons with tube 5, eyes with tube 8, stitching, mouth, patches and nose with tube 1.

3. To make hat, stiffen buttercream to consistency of modeling clay. Roll out and cut a 4" circle. Cut a 2" circle from center to form hat brim. Cut a ¼" strip and wrap around head to form "ledge" for brim. Add tube 234 straw and hair. Hair will help to support brim. Set brim on head. Cut a 3½" circle for hat crown and model to brim. Add a tube 14 rope hat band and belt. With stiffened icing, model pumpkins and corn, grooving for kernels. Add tube 66 husks. Serve Mr. Scarecrow to ten.

Two friendly rivals...

are the centerpiece for an election night party. You'll be surprised at the way they're constructed! Patterns

126

for stiff paper ears for both are in *Celebrate! VI Pattern Book*.

1. For elephant, bake and fill two small wonder mold cakes and two half-egg cupcakes. Ice and toothpick together. Ice ears and insert in head (egg cupcake is placed crossways). Add legs, each made of two marshmallows, and trunk, five small marshmallows. Ice bottoms of feet, then cover elephant with tube 16 stars. Add tube 2 eyes and glaze. Add a paper banner with toothpick staff.

For donkey, bake a cake in the little loafer pan. Toothpick on marshmallow head and neck and small marshmallow nose and legs. Ice thinly overall, add a paper saddle blanket and ears, then cover with tube 16 stars. Pipe tube 13 mane, tube 2 eyes.

2. Sugar-mold stars in candy molds, adding edible glitter for sparkle. Bake, fill and ice a 9″ x 13″ sheet cake. Pipe tube 1D borders and edge with tube 16 shells. Attach stars on mounds of icing, then place animals on cake top. Sheet cake serves 24.

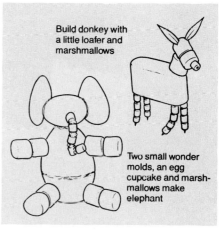

Build donkey with a little loafer and marshmallows

Two small wonder molds, an egg cupcake and marshmallows make elephant

127

Back in training!

TEEN-AGERS are back in classes and training for their chosen sports. Use the easy Color Flow method to decorate these bright cakes for informal parties. The main trim is made in advance—then the cake can be baked and decorated in a hurry!

Bull's-eye!

1. Tape *Celebrate! VI* archer and target patterns to stiff surface, tape wax paper smoothly over them. Outline with tube 1. Flow in heavily with thinned icing. When archer is dry, turn over, lay lengths of thread at ends of bow and outline and flow in again. Attach ends of thread at center of hand, secure with icing and clip off excess. Pipe arrow separately with tube 4 and attach after figure is placed on cake. Over-pipe main lines of archer.

Pipe tree on an ice cream cone. Cover with icing, then pipe random shells on it with tube 16. Pull out "needles" with tube 74.

2. Bake and ice a cake in the long loaf pan. Pipe tube 2 message and do bottom and top tube 17 shell borders. Prop target on cake with popsicle sticks and set tree behind it. Pipe grass with tube 233, then position archer on heavy mounds of icing so he stands out from side of cake. Attach arrow and serve to 16 teen-agers.

Shoot a basket!

This leaping figure is just the right size and proportion to set on an easy-to-serve long loaf cake! Do the figure and balls in the Color Flow method as described at left. When dry, pipe contrasting stripes with tube 55, trim on shoe with tube 1 and over-pipe eye with tube 1s.

1. Bake, fill and ice a long loaf cake. Starting 1½" in from each corner, make two marks 2½" apart, midway on long sides. Make marks 1½" from corners on short sides. Drop string guidelines for lattice and garlands.

2. Pipe tube 8 bulb borders at bottom and top of cake. Pipe zigzag garlands with tube 5, then over-pipe twice with same tube, pausing between pipings to let icing set up. Pipe tube 2 lattice, then edge with tube 2 beading. Ice flat sugar cubes to cake top, pipe a dot of icing on each and set Color Flow figure on them. This exciting cake serves 16.

Go for it!

Catch the action of this agile little gymnast as she floats in mid-air! Do the figure in the Color Flow technique, just as described for the archer. Use *Celebrate! VI* patterns for figure and lettering. When dry, over-pipe eye with tube 1s.

1. Bake, fill and ice a 10" square two-layer cake. For base border, pipe large "C's" with tube 18, then go back and fill in with smaller contrasting "C's" with tube 16. Pipe tube 16 top shell border.

2. Using pattern, mark position of figure on cake top. Transfer message pattern to cake. Do message in the fill-in technique. Outline with tube 1, then fill in, just like Color Flow, with thinned icing. Set figure on cake, raising on high mounds of icing. Serve to 20.

Decorator's secret. When doing Color Flow figures like these, have the thinned icing for flow-in a little thicker than usual. This will allow you to build up the rounded figures in a natural way. After outlining designs, be sure to let the outlines crust before filling in—otherwise colors may bleed.

Things that go o-o-o-o-h! in the night

DELICIOUSLY SCARY and sure to be highlights of halloween celebrations!

The wickedest witch...

poses before a lurid crescent moon.

1. Using *Celebrate! VI* patterns, cut the moon and stars from Roll-out cookie dough and bake. Add a little piping gel to royal icing and outline the cookies, then fill in with thinned icing. (The piping gel makes the outline stick to the cookie.) Attach a popsicle stick to the back of the moon and one star with royal icing.

2. Bake, fill and ice a two-layer 8" square cake. Cover sides with a second coat of icing and mark with a decorating comb. Pipe shell borders at bottom and top with tubes 19 and 17. Attach stars to cake sides, and push in moon and star on cake top. Set witch figure on cake top and serve to twelve trick-or-treaters.

A gaggle of ghosts...

swarm on a hexagon cake! They're fun to figure pipe right on the cake.

1. Cut out the bats from black paper using *Celebrate! VI* pattern. For the tree, clip a branch from a bush, wash and paint with thinned icing.

2. Bake, fill and ice a 12" two-layer hexagon cake. Pipe shell borders with tube 15. Insert tree in cake top. Use Figure piping icing for the ghosts —the cake surface will support the ghosts on the cake sides, the tree will serve as a prop for the one on top. Pipe them with tube 2A, then use tube 2 for the clutching hands. Indent eyes and mouths. Pipe with piping gel and tube 1. Pipe pumpkins with tube 199 puffy stars, add tube 2 stems. Glue bats to tree and frighten 20 halloween party-goers.

Jack-o-lantern cakes...

look just like the real thing!

1. Bake and fill a ball cake, an egg cake and little cakes baked in the egg cupcake pan. Trim off bases of larger cakes for stability. Ice the egg cupcakes with buttercream.

2. Place the larger cakes on wax paper and ice thickly with buttercream. Groove with a spatula, then pat with hands to round out the grooves. Chill for several hours. Pipe tube 105 and 110 stems on wax paper like upright shells. Freeze.

3. With a sharp knife, carefully cut out features on the pumpkins. Remove icing gently. Fill in areas with tube 2 yellow dots and smooth. Now cover the yellow icing with tube 1 yellow piping gel dots. Remove stems from wax paper and attach, upside down, to pumpkins. Let all pumpkins air-dry about eight hours. Then they will be firm enough to arrange on a serving tray. Each large Jack-o-lantern serves twelve.

Decorator's secret. To serve unusually shaped cakes like these, slice vertically in half. Place cut-side down on a plate and slice.

Quick & Pretty sheet cakes

FAST PATTERNS & PERKY TRIMS DRESS UP CAKES IN A JIFFY

USE PANS AND COOKIE CUTTERS to print a pattern on a cake and let you pipe the trim in just minutes. Each of these pretty cakes starts with an iced two-layer 9″ x 13″ sheet cake. Each is easy to serve and makes a striking centerpiece or a very welcome gift. All cakes serve 24.

1. Scrolls and daisies

1. Lightly mark a line with a ruler 3″ in from each long side of the cake top. Continue the marks on short sides. A 3″ round cutter forms the pattern—two rows of four circles on top, plus two circles on each short side. Mark the center of each circle.

2. Pipe a tube 2 message. Tube 16 does all the decorating. Pipe a shell border at base, then colonial scrolls, using marked pattern as accurate guide. Finish with shell-petal daisies, centered with rosettes.

2. Ruffles and rosebuds

Use your 3″ round cutter to mark the cake top as picture shows. First pipe your message with tube 3. Do base border with tube 19 rosettes. Ruffle the outer three-quarters of each circle with tube 104, then complete the circles with tube 19 rosette "rosebuds." Trim with tube 66 leaves.

3. Flowering hearts

With a ruler, lightly mark the cake top into quarters. Use these lines as center guides as you mark the cake with 3″ heart cutters. Use tube 17 for all trim. Pipe borders, then the hearts and scrolls. Garnish with small-to-medium-size drop flowers. (Use flowers you have made ahead and stored.) Finish with tube 65 leaves. This sweet cake is ideal for Valentine's day, an engagement party, or just to make for someone you love.

4. A sunshine cake!

Use boiled icing for this cake. Divide long sides into sixths, short sides into fourths and mark on top edge. Connect the marks diagonally as shown. Mark a circle in the center with a 6″

pan, then press cake with a 2½″ heart cutter. Outline circle and heart with tube 4. Thin the icing with water and fill in areas. Tube 17 pipes the shells that edge the base and circle and outlines the sun rays. Pipe message and beading with tube 2.

5. A cake for a retiree

1. Press a 9″ oval pan on the cake top for pattern. Outline oval with tube 2B in two motions, starting in center of long side of oval and going to center of opposite side—then completing the oval in the same way. Edge with tube 2 beading and write message with same tube.

2. Run a tube 2B line around base of cake, then trim with tube 46 "rickrack". Do shell-motion top border with the same tube. Pipe tube 3 stems and tube 69 leaves, then pull out tube 234 shaggy mums, using stiffened icing.

How to tint colors progressively

Here's how to assure harmonious color schemes for your cakes and do it the quick easy way. Many of the icings on cakes in this book were tinted progressively.

Start with a pastel tint, usually used to ice the cake. Then divide remaining icing into small containers and add varying amounts of food color to each. All the tints will be harmonious, because all start with the same base tint.

Tinting the icing for the Thanksgiving cake

The glowing color scheme for the cake below is an excellent example of the progressive method.

THE ICING FOR COVERING the cake was mixed first. To a full recipe of Snow-white buttercream, we added 18 drops* of Golden Yellow liquid food color. This yellow icing was modified for the other colors of icing.

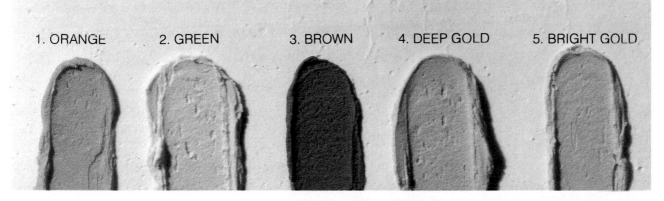

1. ORANGE   2. GREEN   3. BROWN   4. DEEP GOLD   5. BRIGHT GOLD

1. THE ORANGE icing for the bittersweet berries was made by mixing 20 drops of Orange food color into one-half cup of the yellow icing.

2. GREEN ICING for leaves was made by adding eight drops of Leaf Green to one-half cup of yellow buttercream for a soft, warm green.

3. BROWN ICING for cattails and acorns was achieved with cocoa. Make a paste of three tablespoons cocoa, one tablespoon vegetable oil and two tablespoons of water. Add this to one and one-half cups of the basic yellow buttercream.

4. FOR DEEP GOLD color for the oval frame and base border, mix 45 drops (¾ teaspoon) of Golden Yellow liquid color and two teaspoons of the brown icing in one and one-half cups of basic yellow icing. Reserve one-half cup of this tinted icing. With the remaining one cup, mix in an additional two and one-half teaspoons of the brown icing.

5. BRIGHT GOLD for leaves. To the one-half cup of icing reserved from Deep Gold, add 30 drops of Lemon Yellow and mix well.

USE THIS METHOD of mixing colors for many color schemes. Start with a delicate pink—add a few drops of Lemon Yellow for apricot, more Red color for deep pink, and a very little Royal blue for lavender. Or begin with white icing—add a little Leaf Green for pastel green. To the pastel green add Sky Blue for aqua, or Lemon Yellow for a yellow-green.

Decorating the cake

1. Bake, fill and ice with yellow buttercream a two-layer 9″ x 13″ cake. Progressively tint the colors needed for trim and mark top with a 9″ oval pan. Pipe tube 3 message in brown.

2. Use deep gold and tube 2B to outline the frame and pipe base border. Pipe top shell border with tube 17 in the basic yellow icing. Edge oval with tube 3 beading in matching deep gold. Pipe tube 3 stems and tube 10 cattails in brown. Tube 10 acorns trimmed with tube 1 are also brown. Add tube 8 orange berries, tapering tube 6 green leaves and tube 67 bright gold leaves. Repeat the design and colors on corners of cake at base. Serve this glowing cake to 24.

Color do's and don'ts

DO experiment with color. Take out time to tint white icing in various hues and place dabs of them next to each other on white cardboard. You'll be delighted with some of your color schemes. Save them to use on cakes. Experimenting is the only way to attain facility and speed in tinting colors—and it's a lot of fun, too.

DO allow tinted buttercream to rest for an hour or so before putting on a cake. Colors will deepen and you may want to adjust them.

DO keep color trims on a cake at equal intensity or brightness. Bright yellow, bright red and bright blue look right together as shown on page 109. Pastel pink, and apricot blend sweetly in a cake on page 31. White backgrounds set off both schemes.

DON'T use very dark tints of blue, green, maroon or purple on a cake unless you have experimented first— and use these dark colors in very small areas. They may make the cake look dingy and unappetizing.

DON'T tint icing black or grey. These colors do not look edible.

30 drops equal one-half teaspoon

Apple cakes, page 125

FOR THE BOOK CAKE, start with the Color Flow designs. Tape patterns to the book pan, tape wax paper smoothly over and outline with tube 2.

Let outlines crust, then fill in thinly with thinned icing. Do background color first, let set a little, then hearts, leaves and stems. Last of all, flow in red letters. Dry thoroughly. Bake a cake in the book pan, ice and set on cake board. Ice sides thickly and groove with a decorating comb. Pipe a tube 12 line around base of book, attach apple designs and pipe a tube 2B ribbon bookmark. Serves twelve.

FOR THE CUPCAKES, bake a pound cake recipe in egg cupcake pans. Fill, secure two halves with toothpicks and ice with buttercream. Cut about ¾″ off small end of each for stability. Cover with poured fondant. Pipe tube 7 stems and tube 68 leaves.

Use color creatively for distinctive cakes

These four cakes are identical except for color—but don't they look different? Color is the magic that gives each its flair and individuality. Icing for all the cakes and flowers is tinted progressively, except for the white cake. (See page 134.)

A GOLDEN CAKE makes a rich centerpiece for an anniversary or for a man's celebration. Two-tone roses and leaves are just shades deeper than the covering of the cake.

RED ROSES with leaves in a complementary bright green look even more brilliant on a snow-white cake.

Decorate it for the holidays, for a valentine party, or just to please someone who loves red roses!

A PINK AND PRETTY cake for a girl of any age. Deeper pink centers the dainty roses, delicate pastel green leaves set them off.

A SUNNY YELLOW cake is centered with apricot roses and yellow-green leaves. This subtle scheme makes use of closely related colors.

A beautiful border design...

is almost the only trim on these simple cakes. Divide a two-layer 10″ round cake into eighths and mark scallops with a cookie cutter on top and at base.

Here's how to pipe the border. Use double tube 3 string, the upper one centered with a loop, to outline the scallops. Fill with a fan piped with tube 79. Pipe tube 5 balls within the string and tube 5 scrolls and dots between each scallop. Base of cake is edged with tube 19 shells, top with tube 16 rope. Trim cake with tube 124 roses and buds, tube 67 leaves. Serve to 14 guests.

Celebrate!

NOVEMBER AND DECEMBER

Frosted filigree, directions page 141

MAKE SOMEONE HAPPY with cookie treats you've baked and decorated yourself! Gift a little girl with a set of Alice in Wonderland cookies and add the story book too. Trim a chocolate cake with a wreath of jolly Santa cookies to please a boy or his father! And everyone will love these cookie dolls to hang on the Christmas tree. Easy directions are on page 154.

Cookies for *Christmas*

Quick &
Pretty

Center piece Cakes for the Holidays

Grace your holiday table with a cake as radiant as Christmas itself!

Christmas Joy *at left*

Only you will know that this cake can be created very quickly!

1. Bake a two-layer 9″ heart cake. Fill, then cover smoothly with rolled fondant. (Directions are on page 52.) Pipe a few royal icing holly leaves on wax paper with tube 68. Pull out points with a damp artist's brush and dry within a curved form.

2. Transfer *Celebrate! VI* pattern to cake top. Outline design with tube 1 and royal icing. After outlines crust, fill in areas with piping gel. Run a line of tube 17 shells around the base of the cake. Above them, pipe tube 14 zigzag garlands. Add fleurs-de-lis at garland points with the same tube. Finish by attaching holly leaves and adding tube 3 berries. Display your glittering creation to twelve admiring guests.

Decorator's secret. Transfer only the red lines that form the letters to the cake. The green lines and trim on letters are more quickly done freehand.

Frosted Filigree *page 137*

Filigree that seems as fragile as the etching of frost on a winter window frames scarlet poinsettias

1. Pipe the delicate filigree first with egg white royal icing. Tape *Celebrate! VI* pattern for top filigree to the outside of the largest flower former, then tape wax paper smoothly over it. You will need twelve pieces. Pipe lines and dots with tube 2, then sprinkle with edible glitter and dry thoroughly. Pipe the twelve side pieces on Australian crescent nails. Grease the nails with solid white shortening, then pipe the spoke pattern freehand with tube 2. Be sure to leave at least ⅛″ free of piping at base of nail. Sprinkle with edible glitter and dry. Remove the filigree by placing in a warm oven for just a few minutes. Gently push off the nails.

2. Pipe the poinsettias a new way in royal icing. Cover a number 13 nail with a square of wax paper. Hold wide end of tube 101 in center of nail and jiggle your hand slightly as you move out to edge of nail, then back to center to form petal. The nail defines size of flower. Pipe a circle of eight petals, then pipe a second layer of slightly shorter petals on top of them. Add tube 1 green dots in the flower center and add yellow dots on top of them. Dry, then mount on florists' wire stems. Pipe holly with tube 68, pull out points with a damp artist's brush

and dry on and within curved form.

3. Bake and fill a two-layer 12″ round cake, each layer about 2″ high. Cover with buttercream, then poured fondant. Pipe a tube 17 shell border around base of cake. Insert a Flower Spike in the center. Divide cake in twelfths and mark about 2½″ up from base. Make a second series of marks on top edge of cake, midway between first marks.

4. Twist stems of flowers together, wrap with floral tape and insert in Flower Spike. Add a few holly leaves on mounds of icing. Carefully place top filigree pieces on cake, using marks on top edge as guides. Secure each with a few dots of icing. Pipe a tube 2 bow at each mark on side of cake centering "knot" on mark. Attach a side filigree crescent between each bow by piping dots of icing on points of crescent and pressing gently to cake. Finish by adding clusters of holly leaves on mounds of icing. Pipe the berries with tube 3. Serve to 22 guests.

Decorator's secret. Planning ahead will make the final decorating and assembling of any challenging project easy and enjoyable. For this cake, you can pipe the filigree, flowers and leaves days in advance.

Take just a little extra time and care to turn out imaginative treats that add extra cheer to the holidays. Marzipan, recipe page 157, makes all the delectable trims on these creations.

Jolly snowmen

Bake a batch of egg-shaped cupcakes, add marshmallow heads and warm them up with marzipan caps and mufflers!

1. Bake cupcakes in an egg cupcake pan, fill and trim off the wide ends to give them stability. Insert one or two toothpicks in each to make sure the two halves stay together. Cover with boiled icing. Insert a toothpick into a marshmallow and ice for head. When icing has set, thread a miniature marshmallow onto pick for neck, then insert toothpick into body. Figure pipe arms with tube 2A.

2. For caps, form 1″ balls of marzipan, then cut in half. Groove with an orangewood stick. Attach to head with icing. Roll out marzipan thinly, cut ½″ strips and wrap around caps for cuffs. For mufflers, cut ½″ strips of rolled marzipan, wrap around necks, trimming to fit, then attach strips for ends. Brush on egg white to secure cap, cuffs and muffler pieces. Glaze all marzipan with corn syrup glaze. Complete the jolly company by piping tube 3 features and buttons, tube 1 fringe and tube 13 pompons.

Fruit bonbons

Have you ever seen a prettier, more appealing plate of treats? Colorful marzipan fruits make the professional-looking trim.

Bake something Bright for Christmas

1. Tint marzipan, then roll into a cylinder ¾″ in diameter. Cut off ¾″ lengths and roll between your palms into balls. Add grooves for peaches or cherries. For strawberries, form into tapered shape and roll in red-tinted granulated sugar. For bananas, form into cylinders, curve them and pinch ends. Touch up with thinned brown food color. After fruits have set, glaze with corn syrup glaze.

2. Bake a sponge or pound cake in a 1″ deep sheet cake pan. Chill, then slice into two layers with a serrated knife. Fill with jam or buttercream, then cut into 1″ squares. Frost with buttercream, then cover with poured fondant.

Roll out marzipan to about ⅛″ thickness, and roll lightly with a grooved rolling pin for texture. Cut into strips the height of the bonbons and wrap around the candies, brushing end of strip with egg white to secure. Glaze strips. Arrange fruit on bonbons and pipe tube 1 stems and tube 65s leaves.

Dress up a fruitcake

Turn a fruitcake into a glowing gift by adding a wreath of marzipan apples.

1. Model apples, using the same technique as that used for the bonbon trims. Roll out marzipan and cut leaves with the small rose leaf cutter from the Flower Garden set. Lay within curved surface to dry. Glaze fruit and leaves.

2. Brush hot apricot glaze over a ring-shaped fruitcake. (See page 16.) Form a long cylinder of marzipan, roll out and groove with a grooved rolling pin. Cut a strip the height of the cake, and wrap around, securing end with a little egg white. Glaze strip with apricot or corn syrup glaze. Set a fat red candle in the center hole.

Decorator's secret. Always glaze marzipan. The glaze not only gives an attractive shine, but keeps the marzipan fresh and moist. If you haven't worked with marzipan before, experiment with it on pretty trims like these or on a design of your own. Marzipan is very easy to work with and models quickly into realistic forms that taste as good as they look.

Ginger bread!

This year, instead of a gingerbread house, build this fanciful gingerbread tower, ringed with marching animals and dancing children. Construct it easily, right on the Tall Tier stand.

You'll need two batches of the recipe on page 158 (or use your own favorite). There'll be a little left over.

1. Roll dough about ⅛″ thick for all pieces. For round bases on lower tiers, use 14″, 10″, and 16″ cake circles or pans as patterns. Use *Celebrate! VI* pattern for top tier. After circles are on baking sheets, cut a hole in the center of each with a 1¾″ round cutter. Lay *Celebrate! VI* patterns on circles and mark side panel positions with a toothpick. Use patterns for all side panels, elephants, giraffes and small stars, Christmas Cutters for three angels and large star, small People cutters for children and Animal cutters for horses and pigs.

Bake and cool all cookies. Round bases may cool on plates. While still warm, sprinkle with edible glitter.

2. Decorate side panels. Outline with tube 2 and flow in with thinned royal icing. Do the same for all stars. Stir a little piping gel into royal icing and use with tube 1 for trim on all cookie pieces. Let your imagination take over as you pipe outlines, dots, flowers and hearts. Set all aside to dry.

3. Prepare the Tall Tier stand. Use 18″, 14″, 10″ and 8″ plates with round cookie bases on them. Use two 7¾″ columns to separate three lower tiers. Use a 6½″ column between 10″ and 8″ plates. Wrap all columns with gilt ribbon. Flatten the top 2″ of a 10″ long, ¼″ dowel rod by shaving with a sharp knife. Starting 3″ up from other end, wind the rod with five layers of floral tape. Attach large star to flat end with royal icing.

4. Construct the tower with royal icing. On bottom plate, pipe a line of icing on round cookie base where center front panel position is marked. Set panel against it. Pipe a line of icing on one side of panel and on adjacent marked panel position. Set second panel in position. Attach third panel on other side of center front panel. Continue attaching panels,

doing center back last. Construct other two sets of panels the same way. Cover seams and edge bases with tube 16 shells. Pipe icing on dowel rod holding large star below tape. Insert in hole in nut on top plate.

To attach remaining cookies, insert toothpicks into bases, pipe a little icing on them and set cookies against toothpicks.

Gingerbread Santas

Roll out dough about ⅛″ thick, cut the figures out with large People cutters, bake and cool. Outline color areas with tube 2 and royal icing. Thin the icing and flow in the areas. Dry, then pipe tube 13 hair and beard and tube 2 "fur," features and belt detail.

Decorator's secret. To sparkle a cookie after it has cooled, spray lightly with water from an atomizer, sprinkle with edible glitter and dry.

If your cookie sheet is not large enough for the 14″ base circle, bake it on the back of a 16″ cake pan—or bake it in two halves.

Sweet Souvenirs for Christmas

Make these pretty surprises in unexpected shapes for Christmas.

Chocolate Christmas cards

1. Draw foil smoothly over a sideless cookie sheet. Lay giant cookie cutters, as pictured, on the foil.

2. Chop a pound of summer coating into fine chunks for three or four cards this size. Fill the bottom pan of a double boiler with water to a height so that water will not touch top pan. Bring water to a boil, remove from heat and set top pan in position. Pour in the chopped coating. Stir constantly until the coating is about three-quarters melted. Remove top pan, and continue stirring the coating until it is the consistency of mayonnaise.

3. Carefully pour the melted coating into the cookie cutters to a depth of ¼" or more. Place cookie sheet in refrigerator for a half hour. Lift cutter from hardened coating. If coating clings to cutter and foil, pick up cutter, peel off foil and trim edge of candy with a small spatula. Now thin royal icing with piping gel and do message and trim with tube 1.

Decorator's secret. Be careful that no water gets into the coating as it causes discoloration. Cut shiny cardboard into shapes a little larger than the chocolate cards. Attach card to cardboard with a dab of icing, wrap in clear plastic and add a pretty bow.

Lollipop bouquets

Just mold the hard candy recipe on page 159 in Super-flex molds. After the candies are unmolded, make a half-recipe of the hard candy. Dip coffee stirrers into the hot syrup and attach to the backs of the shapes. Lay them on wax paper to cool and harden, then wrap festively.

Pastel delights

1. Flowers and leaves are molded in

146

Super-flex molds. Prepare summer coating. Add ¼ teaspoon lemon, raspberry or peppermint flavor to each ½ pound of yellow, pink or green coating. Mmmm!

2. Striped chocolate mints. First fold a triple thickness of foil into a 12″ square. Bend up all the edges about ½″ to form a pan. Prepare a pound of chocolate coating and a ½ pound of green coating. Add five or six drops of rum butter flavoring to the melted chocolate coating, three drops of peppermint to the green.

Spread half the chocolate coating into the prepared pan. Cover with the green coating, then spread the remaining chocolate coating. Let set up at room temperature, then cut into squares, then triangles. Refrigerate until hardened.

Your-way Cookies

Shape up your own cute quick cookies—just a little imagination, standard cutters, a sharp knife and brightly tinted buttercream will turn out trays of custom cookies to delight the children. Start with a recipe of Roll-out cookies, page 158, then let your own creativity take over. Compose all shapes on the cookie sheet, brushing with water where they touch or overlap.

The angels start with a 2½″ round cookie with side curves cut off to form wings. Add a 1⅜″ round cookie for head. For candles, cut ¾″ strips of dough and trim into holder and candle. The flame is cut with the large violet leaf cutter.

The cute little elf is a 2¼″ round cookie with a 2″ heart cutter hat. Make wagons with 1¾″ strips and 1⅜″ wheels. Snowmen are three round shapes, 2¼″, 1⅜″ and 1.″ Cut ¾″ strips of dough into squares, then cut each square in half to make the triangular hats. Spirals and zig-zags are all done with tube 14, tube 3 does all the other trim.

...and cupcake flowers

Bake your favorite cake recipe in paper cups, then swirl with boiled icing. Turn the cupcake like a flower nail to pipe the poinsettias. First pipe four leaves with tube 74. Use the same tube to pipe the petals, first a circle of eight, then a second circle of four shorter petals. Finish with a center cluster of tube 2 green dots. Top them with yellow dots. Set the little cakes on a serving tray. They're as cheerful as a Christmas card!

Color-me Cookies

Use this quick technique and cutters from your Flower Garden set to make this charming assortment of Christmasy treats.

Start with a recipe of Roll-out cookies, page 158. Divide dough in thirds. Tint one-third green and one-third red by kneading in liquid food colors. Keep dough not in use tightly wrapped in plastic. Now roll out small portions of the dough as you need it to compose the cookies.

Santa heads are made by cutting out red dough with the tulip leaf cutter. Top with a circle of untinted dough cut with the medium rose cutter. Attach shapes by brushing with a little water. Make holly wreaths with a 2" round cutter, center hole cut with small rose cutter. Attach small rose leaves and berries cut with tube 12.

Here are the methods for the other cookies shown. Stockings: cut off a bit from the daffodil cup shape for the leg of the sock. Cut one petal from the small tulip shape for the foot. Poinsettias: set one daffodil petal shape on top of a second. Holly sprigs: three holly leaf shapes with balls of red dough added for berries. Tree ornaments: cut a green tulip leaf shape in two and attach a contrasting half-leaf. "Inset" stars are cut out with the calyx cutter and replaced with untinted stars. The moon-and-star cookies are cut with the medium rose cutter and inset with calyx cutter stars.

These vivid cookies are so attractive they need only a touch of piped trim done with tube 3 or 14.

149

Noel...a radiant bridal masterpiece for a holiday wedding

This breathtaking creation is framed in light! A soft glow illuminates the base of the tiers, picks out the lacy detail of the pillars and beams from the triple bell ornament. This holiday magic is achieved with tiny Christmas tree lights.

Prepare the separators

You will need four tall square pillars, two 14″ round separator plates, four 3″ filigree bells, the petite ornament for between the tiers and the large triple bell ornament. Three 50-light strings of lights were used.

1. For base of cake, cover a sturdy 22″ square cake board with foil and edge with a cake ruffle. Use masking tape to secure an entire string of lights to board, on top of the ruffle. Let lights lie on top of ruffle—tape wire to inner part of board. Tape a second ruffle on top of the lights.

2. Use a needle-nose pliers to remove the stud plates within tops of pillars, leaving holes. Break a small section from top rim of pillar to accommodate wire. Attach pillars to separator plate. Bunch nine lights together with florists' wire to the length of the pillar. Drop lights in pillar, taping to secure at top. Add lights to second pillar, leaving one light free between them. Complete other two pillars the same way. Break a small opening in the top of each bell and insert lights between pillars. You will have ten lights remaining on the string.

3. Tape ruffle to top of separator plate and snap plate in position on top of pillars. Now add lights to triple bell ornament, working on top of separator plate. Cut 18 4″ squares of tulle and bunch each to form a pouf by wrapping center with a short length of florists' wire. Now, using third string of lights, insert a bulb in each heart-shaped opening in ornament frame, then insert a tulle pouf and secure bulb to frame with wire on pouf. With a sharp knife, cut an opening in back of each bell and insert three bulbs in each bell. Insert more tulle poufs in openings of base of ornament, then bunch six bulbs and tape to underside of base. You will have 17 bulbs left over. These, together with ten remaining bulbs from pillars, will surround the upper separator plate.

4. Tape remaining bulbs to top of plate. Leave one bulb free extending from ornament. This will leave sufficient electrical wire to reach from ornament to plate. Tape a second ruffle on top of bulbs around plate.

Decorate the tiers

1. Bake, fill and ice the three two-layer tiers. Base tier is 18″ square, each layer 2″ high. Middle tier is 12″ round, each layer 2″ high. Top tier is 8″ round, each layer 1½″ high. Set base tier on a 20″ foil-covered cake board. Set middle tier on a 13″ cake board, then attach top tier. Divide each side of base tier into sixths. Divide two upper tiers into eighths.

2. On base tier, pipe a tube 32 bottom shell border. Use cross tube 78 to pipe the intricate-looking ruffled garlands. Add tube 3 strings, tube 16 rosettes and a tube 19 reverse shell border at top. Finish with tube 320 fleurs-de-lis at top and side corners.

3. On middle tier, pipe a tube 21 bottom shell border. Do ruffled garlands with tube 78, strings with tube 3, rosettes with tube 16, fleurs-de-lis and big rosettes with tube 320. Add a tube 19 top shell border.

4. On top tier, pipe a tube 19 bottom shell border. Pipe tube 53 garlands and edge with tube 1 loops. Pipe tube 320 fleurs-de-lis at tier top.

5. Assemble tiers at the reception site. Secure base tier, on its board, to prepared ruffle-and-light-trimmed board. Set assembled separator set in position. Set top two tiers on top plate of separator, then set bell ornament on top. Glue satin bows to bells, and trim base of petite ornament between tiers with tulle poufs. Light up this radiant bridal creation. To cut, lift two top tiers off separator, remove separator, then lift base tier off lighted cake board. Double cake boards make this easy. Two lower tiers of Noel serve 230, top tier serves 30.

Decorators secret. Explore the quick effects of the cross tubes—tubes 49 through 54 and tubes 77 and 78. In just one motion they can pipe a triple-ruffled garland. Have a friend help you assemble the tiers. It takes two pairs of hands to hold top ornament out of the way as two upper tiers are set in position.

Candy *from your kitchen!*

SET ASIDE AN EVENING OR TWO
AND GET THE FAMILY TOGETHER
FOR THE FUN OF MAKING CANDY.
WRAP SOME FOR FESTIVE GIFTS,
SAVE SOME FOR HOLIDAY TREATS

Chocolate-dipped peel

Peel of 2 large oranges
2 cups granulated sugar
1 cup water
1½ cups granulated sugar
8 ounces (approximately) milk chocolate

Score oranges into quarters with a sharp knife. Carefully remove peel. Put 6 cups of water in a saucepan, add peel and bring to boiling. Simmer 30 minutes, drain. Repeat the process, then scrape white membrane from peel. Cut into ¼" strips.

Heat the 2 cups of sugar and one cup of water to boiling, stirring to dissolve sugar. Add strips of peel and simmer 45 minutes, stirring frequently. Turn peel into strainer, drain well. Spread 1½ cups of sugar in a sheet pan and roll strips in it to cover. (Left-over sugar may be sifted and re-used.) Straighten strips and lay on wax paper to dry overnight. Break chocolate into small pieces, place in a metal measuring cup and set cup in hot water. Make sure no water touches chocolate. When chocolate is melted, dip peel into cup to coat. Dry by setting undipped ends of peel between the wires of a baking rack.

Pastel divinity

2 cups sugar
½ cup hot water
⅓ cup light corn syrup
¼ teaspoon salt
2 egg whites
1 teaspoon vanilla
½ cup chopped green candied cherries
½ cup chopped red candied cherries
Liquid food coloring

Combine sugar, water, syrup and salt in a saucepan. Bring to a boil, stirring constantly. Cover pan and continue cooking for two minutes. Remove cover and heat without stirring until syrup tests 254°F on a candy thermometer. Meanwhile, beat egg whites until stiff in a large mixer bowl. As soon as syrup reaches 254°F, pour it in a thin stream into egg whites as you continue beating until mixture holds its shape and loses its gloss. Transfer half of mixture into a warm bowl. Add a few drops of red food coloring and the red cherries to half of the candy, green color and green cherries to the other half. Keep candy you are not working with covered with a cloth wrung out of hot water. Drop from a buttered teaspoon onto wax paper to dry. Yield: 1¼ pounds.

Best-ever toffee

1 cup pecans, chopped
¼ cup brown sugar (packed)
½ cup butter or margarine
1 bar (4½ ounces) milk chocolate candy, broken into pieces

Spread pecans in a buttered 8" square pan. Heat sugar and butter to boiling and boil seven minutes, stirring constantly. Immediately spread mixture over nuts. Sprinkle the chocolate pieces over the hot mixture and cover with a baking sheet to contain heat. Spread melted chocolate, let cool a little and spread again, making decorative grooves with a knife. When candy has cooled to warm temperature, cut into 1" squares. Chill until firm. Yield: about 60 squares.

Praline squares

1 cup light brown sugar, lightly packed
¼ cup butter
3 tablespoons milk
2 cups sifted confectioners' sugar
¼ cup chopped pecans
1 teaspoon vanilla extract

Butter an 8" square pan. Combine sugar, butter and milk in a heavy saucepan. Heat to boiling, stirring constantly. Reduce heat and simmer five minutes. Remove from heat and stir in remaining ingredients. Spread into pan and cool until firm. Cut into 1" squares. Cover pan tightly with plastic wrap and chill for several hours, then dip into semi-sweet chocolate (see below). Yield: about 60 centers.

Double chocolate marzipan

4 ounces almond paste
1 egg white
2 cups sifted confectioners' sugar
2 tablespoons cocoa

Place marzipan in a small bowl, set mixer on low speed and break into small pieces. Beat in egg white until smooth, then one cup of the sugar. Turn out on counter and knead in remaining sugar and cocoa. Roll between palms into 1" balls. Set balls on wax paper-covered tray, cover tightly with plastic wrap, chill well. Dip into semi-sweet chocolate. Yield: about 45 centers.

Time-saving method for chocolate-dipped candies.

Heat water in the bottom of a double boiler to boiling. Water should not touch bottom of upper pan. Remove from heat, place top pan in position and pour in about 20 ounces of semi-sweet chocolate morsels. Stir constantly until melted. Insert candy thermometer and stir until thermometer registers 110°F. Remove lower pan, and replace hot with cold water. Set upper pan in position and stir and scrape sides of pan with a rubber spatula until thermometer registers 90°F. Now begin dipping. If temperature drops to 83°F replace cold water with warm.

To dip centers, prepare a dipping tool by bending the tines of a small fork at a 90° angle to the handle. Drop center into chocolate and lift out with the fork. Set on wax paper to dry. You may insert a toothpick into the marzipan centers, dip into the chocolate and stick into styrofoam to dry.

Decorator's secret. Never allow even a drop of water to get into the chocolate. The whole batch will stiffen. Work in a 65° to 70°F room.

Chocolate raisin clusters

To use the last of the chocolate, drop in raisins, stir well and drop by teaspoons onto wax paper to dry.

"She found a little bottle... and tied round the neck was a paper label, with the words 'Drink Me.' "

Re-create Alice, the King and Queen of Hearts, the White Rabbit, Mad Hatter and trio of fearful gardeners in cookie dough and bright-colored icing.

1. Transfer the *Celebrate! VI* patterns to rolled cookie dough (recipe page 158). Bake and cool cookies.

2. Outline the cookies with tube 1 and brown-tinted royal icing. After the out-line has crusted, thin the icing with a little water until it flows easily out of a parchment cone with a tiny cut tip. Fill in the color areas with this thinned icing and allow to dry thoroughly. Now add the details with tube 1. The "roses" growing above the gardeners are tube 135 drop flowers.

Decorator's secret. Transfer just the main lines of the patterns to the baked cookies. As you pipe the details, keep the original pattern in front of you as a reference. Before starting to decorate, mix all the colors you will need and keep in covered small containers. Then fill in all areas of the same color on all cookies at once. Work will go more speedily.

Quick & Pretty Christmas dolls

Use the same techniques for baking and decorating as were used for the "Alice" cookies. Do all outlining and curly hair with tube 2. After flowed-in areas are thoroughly dry, add holly with tube 65, or Christmas balls with tube 3. Thread ribbon through the holes for hanging.

Decorator's secret. After the icing has dried, turn the dolls over and outline and flow in the backs of the cookies. They'll be pretty from any angle! Note that arms, legs and faces are left un-iced.

A wreath of Santas... Quick & Pretty

1. Bake and decorate eight Santa cookies using *Celebrate! VI* patterns and the same techniques as were used for the Alice cookies. Use tube 2 for outlining and features. When the flowed-in areas are dry, add mustache and "fur" borders with tube 14.

2. Bake a two-layer cake in 12" round pans and fill and ice with Chocolate buttercream. Edge the base with tube 19 curved shells, the top with tube 17 shells. Push a candle into the center of the cake and surround with

shells. Arrange the cookies on the cake top. Serve to 22 guests.

Santa reigns at the North Pole
shown on the opposite page

1. First bake and fill the tiers. Base tier is 12" square, two layers. Make sure the layers are about 2" high. Upper tier is a two-layer 8" round. Also bake a cake in the Small Wonder Mold for Santa's body. Ice all smoothly in buttercream. Dip two marshmallows in red thinned icing for legs, and a third in flesh-colored icing for head. Dry. Assemble the tiers on a sturdy cake board with Crystal Clear dividers and a 10" plate. On sides of base tier press tree and star cutters to form design, holly cutter on top of tier. All cutters are from the Christmas set.

2. On base of lower tier, pipe a tube 19 star border. Pipe a tube 17 curved shell border on top edge of tier. Outline marked designs with tube 14, adding decorative rosettes. On upper tier pipe a tube 18 base star border and accent with tube 14 stars. Heap boiled icing on top of tier and sprinkle with edible glitter.

3. Build Santa right on the top tier. Set Wonder Mold cake slightly to rear of tier. Thread a miniature marshmallow for neck, then the iced marshmallow for head on a toothpick and insert in top of Wonder Mold. Pipe belt with tube 45 and add a tube 2 buckle. Attach legs with toothpicks. Stiffen buttercream with confectioners' sugar and hand-model the boots. Secure to legs with icing. Add fluffy "fur" trim around pants, down front and at hem of jacket with tube 14.

Lean a large candy cane against fig-ure, then figure pipe arms with tube 1A, mittens with tube 6. Give Santa a tube 4B cap and tube 2 features. Complete by piping tube 14 mus-tache, beard and hair. Add cuffs and trim on cap with the same tube.

4. Use icing and ribbon bows to secure small and large candy canes to dividers and corners of base tier. Serve to 46 guests.

Recipes for decorators

All have been tested by the Wilton Book Division decorating staff.

We've added a "when to use" note at the end of each recipe to guide you in making a choice. Most of the cakes in this book were iced in Snow-white buttercream, with borders and other trim done in Norman Wilton's boiled icing. Please remember—when making any boiled icing, keep bowl and utensils grease-free. Even a speck of grease will break these icings down.

Another important note: always keep boiled or royal icings covered with a damp cloth as you work.
They crust quickly.

You may use a standard electric mixer for any of the recipes whose yield is four cups or less. Use a heavy-duty mixer, such as Kitchen Aid K5-A for larger recipes. *Never* use a hand-held mixer—it just doesn't have enough power.

You may need to thin or stiffen the icings for some types of piping. To pipe leaves or strings, remove a portion of icing from the batch and add a little piping gel or white corn syrup. (Note: Chocolate buttercream does not need to be thinned for leaves or string.) Experiment until you have a consistency that flows easily. For most flowers, stiffen the icing with confectioners' sugar. Here again, experiment for correct amount.

Wilton snow-white buttercream

  ⅔ cup water
  4 tablespoons meringue powder
  1¼ cups solid white shortening, room temperature
  11½ cups confectioners' sugar, sifted
  ¾ teaspoon salt
  ¼ teaspoon butter flavoring
  ½ teaspoon almond flavoring
  ½ teaspoon clear vanilla flavoring

Combine water and meringue powder and whip at high speed until peaks form. Add four cups sugar, one cup at a time, beating after each addition at low speed. Alternately add shortening and remainder of sugar. Add salt and flavorings and beat at low speed until smooth. May be stored, well covered, in refrigerator for several weeks, then brought to room temperature and rebeaten. Yield: 8 cups. Recipe may be cut in half or doubled.

When to use. This is a pure white, versatile and delicious icing. We recommend it both for covering the cake and piping borders.

Wilton chocolate buttercream

  ⅓ cup butter
  ⅓ cup solid white shortening
  ½ cup cocoa
  ½ cup milk
  1 pound confectioners' sugar, sifted
  5 tablespoons cool milk or cream
  1 teaspoon vanilla
  ⅛ teaspoon salt

Cream butter and shortening together with an electric mixer. Mix cocoa and ½ cup milk and add to creamed mixture. Beat in sugar, one cup at a time, blending well after each addition and scraping sides and bottom of bowl frequently. Add cool milk, vanilla and salt and beat at high speed until light and fluffy. Keep icing covered with a lid or damp cloth and store in refrigerator. Bring to room temperature and rebeat to original consistency. Yield: 3⅔ cups.

When to use. This makes a delicious, light chocolate-colored icing, ideal for icing the cake. To pipe flowers, mix one cup of confectioners' sugar with one cup of the finished icing. For a darker flower, add three tablespoons of cocoa and ⅔ cup of confectioners' sugar to one cup of icing.

Norman Wilton's boiled icing —meringue

Mixture One
  7 ounces granulated sugar
  ⅛ teaspoon cream of tartar
  4 ounces water

Mixture Two
  1 cup warm water
  3 ounces meringue powder
  1½ pounds confectioners' sugar
  ½ cup white corn syrup

Combine ingredients in *Mixture One* in a heavy saucepan and cook to 240°F. Brush sides of pan with a wet pastry brush several times while heating to prevent crystallization.

Meanwhile, prepare *Mixture Two.* Whip warm water and meringue powder about seven minutes or until fluffy. Add confectioners' sugar and whip at low speed about three minutes. Slowly pour hot syrup (*Mixture One*) into batch and whip at high speed until light and very fluffy. Now add the corn syrup and whip about three minutes. Use immediately or put into a tightly closed container to keep for weeks.

Use paddle attachment to beat to original consistency. Yield: 12 cups, enough to trim a large tiered wedding cake. You may double or triple the recipe, but use a commercial mixer—a household mixer is not big enough.

When to use. "Not for icing the cake, but my favorite for flowers and borders. The corn syrup keeps it moist and gives a wonderful gloss. I've given demonstrations with this icing when it was ten weeks old! It's very easy to pipe with."—*Norman Wilton*

Wilton boiled icing — egg white

2 cups granulated sugar
½ cup water
¼ teaspoon cream of tartar
4 egg whites, room temperature
1½ cups confectioners' sugar, sifted

Boil granulated sugar, water and cream of tartar to 240°F. Brush sides of pan with warm water to prevent crystals. Brush again halfway through, but do not stir. Meanwhile, whip egg whites 7 minutes at high speed. Add boiled sugar mixture slowly, beat 3 minutes at high speed. Turn to second speed, gradually add confectioners' sugar, beat 7 minutes more at high speed. Rebeating won't restore texture. Yield: 3½ cups.

When to use. This marshmallow flavored icing is fine for covering the cake. Do not use for borders or flowers.

Figure piping icing

1½ cups granulated sugar
⅓ cup water
¼ teaspoon cream of tartar
2 tablespoons meringue powder
⅓ cup lukewarm water
⅝ cup confectioners' sugar, sifted

Cook the first three ingredients to 236°F. While this mixture is cooking, beat meringue powder with lukewarm water until it peaks. Add confectioners' sugar slowly, then beat at medium speed until blended.

Now pour the cooked mixture into meringue mixture and continue beating at medium speed until peaks form. Wrap the bowl with towels wrung out of cold water to cool the icing while you are beating. The quicker the icing is cooled, the better it is. (Note: a heavy duty mixer is needed.) Use immediately.

When to use. This icing is the choice of experts for piping upright figures.

Marzipan

1 cup almond paste (8-ounce can)
2 egg whites, unbeaten
3 cups confectioners' sugar
½ teaspoon vanilla or rum flavor

Knead almond paste by hand in a bowl. Add egg whites and mix well. Continue kneading as you add sugar, one cup at a time, and flavoring, until marzipan feels like heavy pie dough. Cover with plastic wrap, then place in a tightly covered container in the refrigerator. Keeps for months.

To tint, knead in a drop of liquid food color at a time.

To roll out, dust work surface and rolling pin with confectioners' sugar.

To glaze marzipan pieces, combine ½ cup corn syrup and one cup water, heat to boiling and brush on. This gives a soft shine. For a high gloss, use just one or two tablespoons water with ½ cup corn syrup.

To put pieces together, brush one lightly with egg white, then fix to second with a turning motion.

When to use. Marzipan is indispensable for decorating in the Australian method. Use it also for modeling life-like fruits and stand-up figures. It's fun and very easy to handle.

Rolled fondant

½ ounce gelatin
¼ cup water
2 pounds confectioners' sugar, sieved three times
½ cup glucose

¾ ounce glycerine
2 tablespoons solid white shortening
2 or 3 drops clear flavoring liquid food color, as desired

Heat gelatin and water in a small pan until just dissolved. Put sieved sugar in a large bowl and make a depression in the center. Add shortening, glucose and glycerine to the dissolved gelatin and heat until shortening is just melted. Mix well. Pour mixture into depression in sugar and mix with your hands to a dough-like consistency. Transfer to a smooth surface covered with nonstick pan release and lightly dusted with cornstarch and knead until smooth and pliable. Add flavoring and color while kneading. If too soft, knead in a little sieved confectioners' sugar. If too stiff, add boiling water a drop at a time.

Use immediately or store in an airtight container at room temperature for up to a week. If storing longer, refrigerate and bring to room temperature before kneading and rolling out on work surface thinly coated with nonstick pan release and dusted with cornstarch. Recipe will cover an 8" x 3" square or a 9" x 3" round cake.

When to use. Give yourself a little time to practice and you'll find you can cover a cake with rolled fondant in just a few minutes. It gives a beautiful satin-smooth finish.

Wilton royal icing — egg white

3 egg whites, room temperature
1 pound confectioners' sugar, sifted
½ teaspoon cream of tartar

Combine ingredients, beat at high speed 7 to 10 minutes. Dries quickly—keep covered. Rebeating will not restore consistency. Yield: 3 cups.

When to use. This is *the* icing for lace, lattice and fine stringwork. It has the necessary strength for free-standing ornaments. Dries too hard for covering the cake.

Wilton royal icing — meringue

- 3 level tablespoons meringue powder
- 3½ ounces warm water
- 1 pound confectioners' sugar, sifted
- ½ teaspoon cream of tartar

Combine ingredients, mixing slowly, then beat at high speed for 7 to 10 minutes. Keep covered with a damp cloth, icing dries quickly. To restore texture, rebeat. Yield: 3½ cups.

When to use. Use for the same purposes as royal icing—egg white.

Wilton quick poured fondant

- 4½ ounces water
- 2 tablespoons white corn syrup
- 6 cups confectioners' sugar
- 1 teaspoon almond flavoring

Combine water and corn syrup. Add to sugar in a saucepan and stir over low heat until well-mixed, lukewarm and just thin enough to be poured. Stir in flavor and color, if desired.

To cover cake, ice smoothly with buttercream and let icing crust. Place cake on cooling rack with a cookie sheet beneath it. Pour fondant over iced cake, flowing from center and moving out in a circular motion. Excess fondant can be reheated and poured again. Yields 4 cups—covers an 8″ cake.

When to use. This icing gives a glossy, grease-free surface that sets off delicate trim beautifully. Continental cakes and petits fours are usually covered with poured fondant.

Chocolate quick poured fondant

Follow recipe for Quick Poured Fondant, but increase amount of water by 1 ounce. After it is heated, stir in 3 ounces of melted, unsweetened chocolate, then add flavoring.

Stabilized whipped cream

- 1 teaspoon unflavored gelatin
- 2 tablespoons cold water
- 1 cup heavy whipping cream (at least 24 hours old and very cold)
- 2 tablespoons confectioners' sugar
- ½ teaspoon vanilla

Add gelatin to cold water in a small metal or pyrex cup. Set in a small pan of boiling water and heat until gelatin dissolves and looks clear (do not stir). Cool gelatin to room temperature. Make sure beaters and bowl are very cold, then whip cream to medium consistency. Pour dissolved gelatin into center all at once and continue beating. Add confectioners' sugar and vanilla. Beat until cream stands in peaks. Yield: 2 cups.

When to use. Covers a cake quickly and easily. Use large tubes for fluffy borders. Refrigerate a whipped cream-decorated cake, and serve no later than the next day.

Roll-out cookies

- 1¼ cups butter
- 2 cups sugar
- 2 eggs
- 5 cups flour
- 1 teaspoon baking powder
- 1 teaspoon salt
- ½ cup milk
- ¼ teaspoon grated orange peel

Cream butter and sugar together, then add eggs and beat until fluffy. Sift dry ingredients together and add alternately to creamed mixture with milk. If mixture is too sticky, add a little more flour.

Roll dough on floured surface and cut. Bake on ungreased cookie sheet in 375°F oven 8 minutes or until edges are light golden brown. Yield: about 4 dozen large cookies.

When to use. Cookies made with this recipe hold their shape very well, and are ideal for decorating. Try rolling the dough on wax paper, cutting out and removing scraps. Slide paper onto cookie sheet and bake.

Grandma's gingerbread

- 5 to 5½ cups all-purpose flour
- 1 teaspoon baking soda
- 1 teaspoon salt
- 2 teaspoons ginger
- 2 teaspoons cinnamon
- 1 teaspoon nutmeg
- 1 teaspoon cloves
- 1 cup shortening
- 1 cup sugar
- 1¼ cups unsulphured molasses
- 2 eggs, beaten

Thoroughly mix flour, soda, salt and spices. Melt shortening in large saucepan. Add sugar, molasses, and eggs; mix well. Cool slightly, then add four cups dry ingredients and mix well.

Turn mixture onto lightly floured surface. Knead remaining dry ingredients by hand. Roll dough to ⅛″ thickness. Cut out pieces with cutters or knife. Place on greased cookie sheets. Bake at 375°F for 8 to 10 minutes. Cool on cookie sheets a few minutes, remove and cool completely on rack.

When to use. Perfect for gingerbread houses and cookie ornaments.

Wilton gum paste

- 1 heaping tablespoon glucose
- 3 tablespoons warm water
- 1 tablespoon Gum-tex™ or tragacanth gum
- 1 pound confectioners' sugar (or more)

Heat glucose and water till just warm. Mix Gum-tex™ with 1 cup of the sugar and add to glucose mixture. Mix well. Gradually knead in enough sugar until you have used ¾ pound. Gum paste handles best when aged, so store in a plastic bag at least overnight, then break off a piece and work in more sugar until pliable but not sticky. Always keep the portion you are not working with well-covered. To store several weeks or more, place in air-tight plastic bag, then second bag or sealed container and refrigerate. Bring to room temperature before using. May be frozen.

To tint, knead in a little paste color.

For flat pieces, roll a small piece on a cornstarch-dusted surface and cut.

To mold, follow directions that come with the molds.

When to use. This is a very pliable mixture that can be rolled very thin. Use it whenever you want perfect fine details in a figure, or the most delicate flowers.

Philippine gum paste

  2 envelopes (2 tablespoons)
    unflavored gelatin
  ⅔ cup water
  2¼ pounds confectioners' sugar
    (approximately)

Pour gelatin over water in the top half of a double boiler. Cook about four minutes over boiling water until clear. Cool to lukewarm. Put sugar into a large bowl and pour in gelatin-water mixture. Stir with a spoon, then turn out onto counter. Sugar will not be completely mixed. Knead vigorously until smooth and elastic. You may use immediately. Keep covered with a damp cloth while working. Recipe

may be cut in half.

To store at room temperature, wrap in a tightly closed plastic bag, then in a second bag. It will remain useable for a week. To store for a longer period, refrigerate, then bring to room temperature.

To tint, knead in a little paste color.

To roll, dust work surface and rolling pin with cornstarch.

To mold, dust molds lightly with cornstarch.

When to use. This recipe produces a very strong, quick drying product. It's especially well suited for large panels or constructed ornaments.

Hard candy

  2 cups granulated sugar
  ⅔ cup water
  ¼ teaspoon cream of tartar
  Food color (by the drop)
  1 teaspoon Hard Candy Flavor

Combine water, sugar and cream of tartar in saucepan and bring to a boil over high heat, stirring constantly. When it begins to boil, stir in coloring,

then insert candy thermometer and stop stirring. Continue cooking over high heat, occasionally wiping sides of pan and thermometer with wet pastry brush.

It will take 12 to 15 minutes for candy to cook, but check thermometer often. When it reaches 280°, turn down to low heat to avoid burning. Stir in flavoring. When candy reaches 300°F, remove from heat and pour into greased molds.

This recipe makes about 50 small shapes. To make more, repeat, rather than doubling recipe.

To mold, lightly grease molds with vegetable oil, place them on foil-lined cookie sheets and pour in hot syrup.

To unmold, let candy cool about 15 minutes in refrigerator, or until it hardens. Turn molds upside-down and pop candy out by pressing back of molds lightly with thumbs.

When to use. Always use Super-Flex or metal molds and make sure they are well coated with vegetable oil.

Serving charts for two-layer party cakes

These suggestions are for dessert-sized portions of two-layer cakes. If your cake is a single layer, cut number of servings in half. Most one-mix cakes of any shape serve twelve.

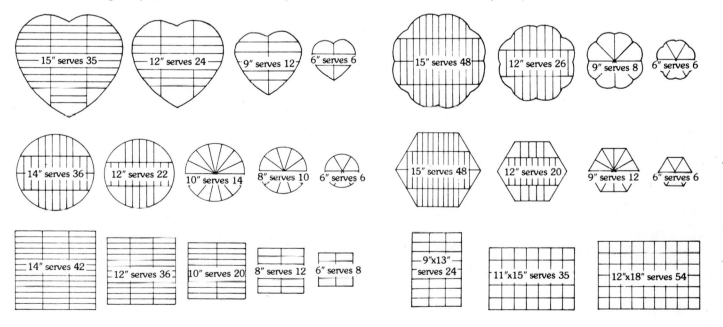

15" serves 35   12" serves 24   9" serves 12   6" serves 6   15" serves 48   12" serves 26   9" serves 8   6" serves 6

14" serves 36   12" serves 22   10" serves 14   8" serves 10   6" serves 6   15" serves 48   12" serves 20   9" serves 12   6" serves 6

14" serves 42   12" serves 36   10" serves 20   8" serves 12   6" serves 8   9"x13" serves 24   11"x15" serves 35   12"x18" serves 54

Index